THE "D" FORCE (MESOPOTAMIA)

IN THE GREAT WAR.

THE "D" FORCE
(MESOPOTAMIA)
IN
THE GREAT WAR

The Naval & Military Press Ltd

Published by
The Naval & Military Press Ltd
5 Riverside, Brambleside, Bellbrook
Industrial Estate, Uckfield, East Sussex,
TN22 1QQ England

Tel: +44 (0) 1825 749494
Fax: +44 (0) 1825 765701

www.naval-military-press.com
www.military-genealogy.com

and

The Imperial War Museum, London
Department of Printed Books
www.iwm.org.uk

To the Honoured Memory

of

Dear Friends and Former Pupils

Whose Bones lie scattered

over the

Sands and Swamps of Irak.

ASH,
 ALDERSHOT.
  NOVEMBER, 1926.

CONTENTS.

THE "D" FORCE (MESOPOTAMIA) IN THE GREAT WAR.

Chapter I.

NEUTRALITY IN WAR, AND WHY TURKEY WAS UNABLE TO REMAIN NEUTRAL.

Whether any country can retain the power and will to preserve its neutrality in a War depends to a great extent on the geographical position of that country. In the Great War none of the belligerents cared a straw whether, for instance, the South and Central American Republics were neutral or not. And it would have been far better, in the long run, for France and England, and for Europe generally, if the United States had remained neutral, and kept out of the War. The result would have been much more satisfactory, to the French and English Armies and to their gallant commanders, who are now invited to believe that the War was *not* won by the Marne, or the Aisne, or the Somme, or Ypres, or Verdun, but by the capture of the St. Mihiel salient.

A country which is so situated as to have the power of influencing the military action of any of the belligerents, or of acting as a corridor for the passage of supplies to them, will be faced with many difficulties in the interpretation of the laws of neutrality, and will be subjected to heavy pressure by interested powers. In the Great European War the position of Spain and Portugal was too remote from the centre of activities to give them a direct interest in the struggle. Still, some ports and harbours on the east coast of Spain served as safe and convenient bases for German submarines ; and some merchants, of Barcelona, Valencia, and Malaga, made handsome profits out of their neutrality. Portugal, the oldest continental ally of England, took an active part in the War as it progressed ; but, even with the best intentions, her influence on the final result cannot be said to have been pre-ponderant.

Coming to the other European neutrals, Holland, Scandinavia, Switzerland, and the Balkan States : their attitude was of greater interest than that of the Iberian Peninsula, since they were all in positions to influence directly the course of the War. From the commencement of hostilities the probability of their entry into the War was widely discussed ; and their policy was of vital importance to both groups of belligerents. Strategically, they offered advantageous positions from which one belligerent could have attacked the naval and military forces of the other ; economically, they provided inlets for supplies to combatants.

The neutrality of Holland and Scandinavia was of tremendous value to Germany, chiefly on economic grounds. This is why the German Emperor expressed to Holland his Imperial admiration for the manner in which she upheld the difficult and dangerous part of neutral. To England and France, Dutch hostility would have been more beneficial than Dutch neutrality ; and this is why William, while trampling underfoot the neutrality of Belgium, treated that of Holland as something praiseworthy and sacred.

The value of the neutrality of Switzerland (and Italy, at the beginning of the War) is more debatable. Strategically, it would have been (with Italy) of immense assistance on either side, standing midway between the North Sea neutrals and the Eastern Mediterranean group.

It is more difficult to attach a precise value to the neutrality of the Balkan States, owing to the complexity of Balkan interests. But there was one outstanding feature in this situation ; namely, they could control the routes by which neutral commerce reached Russia, and by which the bulk of Russian produce was carried to the rest of Europe.

It is interesting to note that the situation in South-Eastern Europe, with regard to neutrality, was the exact converse of the position in North-Western Europe. Dutch and Scandinavian neutrality exactly suited Germany's interests ; but Balkan neutrality would not suit her at all. So she brought the greatest pressure to bear on Turkey, who controlled the entrance to the Black Sea ; and she ultimately persuaded the Ottoman to discard the dull mantle of neutrality for a shining armour of German manufacture.

The attitude of Germany to the principles of neutrality would have been comic had it not been Teutonic. Dutch neutrality was a matter for fulsome admiration ; Belgian neutrality was an object of savage and relentless hostility ; while Turkish neutrality had the mailed fist in its face.

In the first three months of the Great War, Germany had determined the attitude of two countries whose special interest it was to remain neutral. In the prosecution of her political designs, her influence had been established in Belgium and Turkey, at Antwerp and Stamboul.

This was no new situation to the student of European History. Time and again a dominant military power has attempted to consolidate into one Empire the countries which lie along the greatest trade route connecting Eastern and Western markets. Of this trade-route, Antwerp and Constantinople are the termini ; linked together by the river systems of the Rhine and Danube. This is the land route ; as opposed to the sea route ; *its* termini at London and Suez, with the British stepping stones, Gibraltar and Malta, on its line of communications. From Suez and Constantinople the routes stretch out eastwards, to India and China, through the Red Sea and the Indian Ocean ; and, by land, through Asia Minor and Persia, even as it was followed by the armies of Alexander the Great, twenty-three centuries ago. It had been the ambition of Louis XIV to create such an Empire, but he was stopped by Marlborough. The great Napoleon had covered a good part of the way to it, when he was held up by Nelson and Abercrombie ; while we may say of the German Emperor, whose ambition tempted him to start on the same course, that he has been " left at the post " ; having got no further than Holland on the way.

The fulfilment of William's policy required German control of Holland and Belgium in the West ; and, in the East, the establishment and development of a political system which would enable him to exercise predominant influence at Constantinople. This was to be the first step in the " Drang nach Osten," the pressure eastwards ; and German statesmen reckoned that the design would be complete in 1912. Turkish Armies, drilled and armed by Germany, seemed to dominate the Balkans, when two events occurred which changed the whole situation ; causing Germans and pro-Germans to stare and gasp and gnash their teeth. Italy came down on Turkish territory in North Africa, like a steam hammer on a band-box ; and the " Christian " States in the Balkan Peninsula combined against Turkey, for the first time in their existence, and simply walked over the German-trained Ottoman troops. Italy snapped her fingers at the Triple Alliance (with Austria and Germany) ; Turkish influence disappeared from the Balkan Peninsula ; Roumania turned her back on Germany, and began to make overtures to the Franco-Russo-English Entente. The Czar's eldest daughter came to Roumania, to see whether she thought well of the Crown Prince as a husband ; but, in an unlucky moment for herself, she was not pleased with him ; and,

4

as she went on board the Czar's yacht in Constanzia, it is related that an old gipsy warned her of her terrible fate.*

The expansion of Servia had cut off the German Powers from the direct route to Salonika and Constantinople. Turkey was beaten; crippled, politically and' financially; and clean cut off from direct communication with Germany. Therefore, the first object of Germany in the Great War was to regain her control of the Balkans, and to make good her connection with Turkey, who was to be subordinated to German interests until the moment had arrived for the occupation of Constantinople and the letting loose of the Teutonic flood across Asia Minor and Anatolia, from the Ægean Sea to the Persian Gulf.

The nature of Germany's interests in these regions is reflected in the ambitious project of the Baghdad Railway. At first appearance this would seem to be an ordinary commercial enterprise, in which the capital is found by a commercially progressive nation, for the development of a country which had no industrial enterprise. But the project stood for much more than this. Its real object was the establishment of German control over Asia Minor and Mesopotamia. The Baghdad Railway was the outward and visible sign of Germany's political and financial control over Turkey. Germany's unconcealed intention was to establish colonies in the territories along the track of the railway. This was publicly stated by Von der Goltz, the able organiser of the newly-modelled Turkish Army. Turkish finances were determined by the demands of the Baghdad Railway scheme; large sums were earmarked to remunerate German capitalists for their outlay, and were derived chiefly from increased customs' duties.

This great enterprise was bound to influence the foreign relations of Turkey. Because, in the first place, this railway in German hands meant competition with Russian and English trade. Germany had raised her already high tariff against Russian goods in Europe, and she was England's keenest and severest competitor. Thus, the economic rivalry between these Powers, which was a determining factor in the great European struggle, was transferred, with its accompanying political friction, to the whole wide region stretching from the Bosphorus to Basra. The coming event of the completed design cast its shadow over the Middle East. There was a concentration of the rival interests in Persia, a country immediately affected by the Railway scheme. Backed by Germany, Turkey took advantage of Russia's internal troubles after the disastrous Manchurian Campaign, to advance beyond her frontier and occupy important districts in Western Persia, directly south of the Russian frontier. But Russia

*P. Gilliard. " Le Tragique Destin de Nicolas II et de sa Famille."

and England had long established commercial interests in Persia; and, in the face of the threatened German advance into Mesopotamia, they were compelled to take suitable measures for the maintenance of these interests. They well knew that if Turkey, with Germany at her back, was once established in Western Persia, high tariffs and discriminating rates would be employed to strangle Russian and English commerce, and to open for Germany the monopoly of a rich and profitable market. This is why, when Turkey placed herself on the side of Germany in the Great War, a Russian force invaded Armenia, a country whose position dominates the Mesopotamian region; and an Expeditionary Force had to be sent from India to occupy the head of the Persian Gulf, the chief outlet for the trade of the Mesopotamian region.

The Baghdad Railway scheme had very important bearing on the strategic and economic position of India. It provided for a railway which was intended to connect the Bosphorus and the western coast of Asia Minor with the Persian Gulf; and, later on, *via* Persia, with Karachi. The first German concession was obtained in 1888, for the construction of the Anatolia section, to Konieh. Ten years later, the Emperor William made his famous visit to Constantinople, and laid the foundation of an eternal German friendship with the Sultan, Abdul Hamid. At this time it was generally reported in the Mussulman world, and the report was believed in Eastern Turkey,* that William had become a Mohammedan; and it was considered necessary that a Government order, or Firman, should be published, not to deny the rumour, but to threaten with severe punishment anybody who should venture to make jests about a certain ancient ceremony through which all converts to Islam have to pass before they can be reckoned as orthodox Mussulmans.

Anyhow, the result of the friendship between William and Abdul Hamid was the concession for the construction of a railway from Konieh to the Persian Gulf. Afterwards, conventions were made for the completion of the scheme in three sections. The first from Konieh to Eregli, was finished in the end of 1904. The second section, which had immense engineering difficulties to overcome, ran from Eregli to El Kelif. The third section was to take the line all the way to Baghdad. The agreement for its construction, together with the privilege of constructing German harbours at Alexandretta (Iskanderoon) and Basra, was signed in 1911. The whole Railway was to be finished by 1917.

---

*In the early part of the year 1904, Colonel Hassan Bey, commanding an Infantry Regiment in Baghdad, became very indignant with me for refusing to believe this rumour and for laughing at it.

The last section was to run from Baghdad to Basra and the Persian Gulf. Let us here pause a moment to note what this meant. It would have placed at the disposal of the greatest military power in the world a most vital line of communication from Europe to India and the East, a line very nearly following the track of Alexander the Great to the Indus. Thus the enterprise would most directly affect Indian interests ; for with German interests established on the Tigris, and thereby exercising pressure on Persia and the Persian Gulf, India's political relations would have to be adjusted to meet the changed situation. A great British statesman†· said at the time : " It is the intention of His Majesty's Government to maintain the *status quo* in the Persian Gulf, and its maintenance is incompatible with the occupation by any Power of a port in those waters."

---

† Mr. (now Lord) Balfour.

Chapter II.

THE RUPTURE BETWEEN ENGLAND AND TURKEY.

For the three months which followed the outbreak of the Great War in the beginning of August, 1914, England did everything in her power to avoid a conflict with Turkey. It is no exaggeration to state that there has never been a case in history in which a great Power like the British Empire showed such patience, forbearance, and even meekness, in the most trying circumstances, as England showed towards Turkey at this period.

His Majesty, the Emperor of India, our most gracious King George, had one hundred millions of Mohammedan subjects ; while the Sultan of Turkey ruled over only eighteen millions, and twelve millions were under the rule of the French Republic. Yet the Emperor George and his statesmen suffered not only the unfriendliness, but the insults of Turkey, until at last even British good nature and patience could no longer stand the strain.

Why war took place between British India and Turkey is very clearly set forth in a Press *communique* issued at Simla, the headquarters of the Indian Government, on October 30th, 1914. The causes of the War were given as follows :—

" The attitude adopted by the Turkish Government in regard to the German men-of-war, the *Goeben* and *Breslau*, aroused great misgivings in London, Paris and Petrograd. These ships were flying from the French and British Fleets in the Mediterranean ; and took refuge in the Dardanelles, where, by the rules of international law, and under Turkish Treaties, they should either have been laid up by the Turkish Government, their crews not being repatriated until the close of the War, or made to leave for the open sea at the end of twenty-four hours. Instead of this, the ships were allowed to remain in shelter and to exercise belligerent rights on a French ship ; then it was suddenly announced that they had been purchased by Turkey, who retained the German crews, and dismissed the British admiral from his exclusive command of the Turkish Fleet. At the same time the passage of the Dardanelles was sown with mines, and all the British merchant vessels, in these waters, or coming through from the Black Sea, were held up ; first, on the pretence that their cargoes were wanted for troops whom Turkey was mobilising, and then that the presence of mines rendered it unsafe for vessels to proceed. This was not only a totally unjustifiable interference, on the part of a neutral state, with the trade of Great Britain, involving both shippers and merchants in heavy loss ; but it paralysed the movements of all British shipping in the Black Sea, amounting at the time to sixty or seventy vessels ; since not only was it impossible to get through into the Mediterranean, but there was nothing to prevent the *Goeben* and *Breslau* from passing into the Black Sea and destroying all the shipping collected there. The Dardanelles were now closed, in defiance of International Treaties.

"Another reason for grave disquietude has been the unfriendly treatment, by responsible Turkish officials in Baghdad and Mesopotamia, of British subjects, and the open incitement of the population, by Turkish official circles, against Great Britain and her Allies.

"Notwithstanding all this provocation, His Majesty's Government intimated that if Turkish were substituted for German crews on the *Goeben* and *Breslau*, if British merchant shipping were not impeded, and if Turkey would honourably carry out the duties of a neutral state, not only would all these irregularities and hostile acts be overlooked, but a solemn and written guarantee would be given that Great Britain would scrupulously respect the independance and integrity of the Ottoman Empire. Furthermore, assurances were given that, at the conclusion of Peace, Great Britain would see that no conditions were laid down which would impair that independance and integrity, and economic conditions of a character favourable to Turkey would be obtained.

"In spite of these assurances, the attitude of Turkey towards Great Britain became increasingly provocative.

"Evidence continued to reach His Majesty's Government of military preparations in Syria, which could have had no other purpose than to facilitate an attack on Egypt, and of active propaganda carried on by Turkish and German agents among the Arabs in the region adjoining the Egyptian frontier. The Mosul and Damascus Army Corps have, since their mobilisation, been constantly sending troops south, preparatory for an invasion of Egypt and the Suez Canal from Akabah and Gaza. A large body of Bedouin Arabs has been called out and armed to assist in this venture. Transport has been ordered and roads have been prepared up to the frontier of Egypt. Mines have been despatched to be laid in the Gulf of Akabah, to protect the force from naval attack ; and the notorious Sheikh Aziz Shawish, who has been so well known as a firebrand in raising Muslim feeling against Christians, has published and disseminated through Syria and India inflammatory documents urging Mohammedans to fight against Great Britain."

9

So now we have, on one side, the British Empire, which saved Europe, on two remarkable occasions,[†] at least, from what would have been a cruel and blasting tyranny; which saved Turkey herself, on two other occasions,[‡] from ruin and annihilation; and which has spread the blessings of civilisation and peace to the ends of the earth. On the other side we have the Ottoman Empire; a standing camp called a state, which introduced into Europe military music, cockroaches, and the common louse.

It is doubtful whether Turkey could ever have been induced to fight against England had England not been on the side of Russia, the hereditary and deadly enemy of the Ottoman. The average western European can form no idea of the depth of mutual hatred which has long existed between Turkey and Russia. There is nothing like it in any other two countries in the world; the bad feeling between France and Germany, compared with the hatred between Turkey and Russia, is as vinegar compared with vitriol. In the Russo-Turkish War of 1877-78, the wounded Turks and Russians in Lady Strangford's hospitals fought and tore and bit and mangled each other like dogs. Therefore, when Turkey knew that England had gone on the side of the " Moskoff," she felt that the time had again come to " upset the camp-kettles and pluck up the horse-tails."[*] The anti-Russian feeling of the Turk was Germany's trump card, which she certainly played for all it was worth.

The Turkish Army.

The great German strategist, Von der Goltz, had undertaken the organisation and administration of the Ottoman Army. The problem which he had to solve was this : Given an army of 900,000 men, to organise, arrange and distribute it in suitable positions for either standing on the defensive or assuming the offensive on three different and widely-separated fronts, while at the same time assuming the direct offensive on a fourth front. The three former fronts were the Balkans, the Caucasus, and Mesopotamia ; the fourth front being that towards the Suez Canal and Egypt.

In accordance with the given conditions, Von der Goltz divided the whole of the Turkish military forces into thirteen[§] Army Corps, arranged in four groups, corresponding to the four fighting fronts.

The First Army Corps had its headquarters at Constantinople, and its three divisions at Constantinople, Hademkoi, and Skutari. The Second Army Corps was at Adrianople, with two of its divisions at Adrianople and Mustafa Pasha, and the third at Kirki Killesi.

[†]1704 and 1815.   [‡]1856 and 1878.
[*]Turkish expression, from the Jannisaries, for preparation and declaration of war.
[§]Later on the 14th and 15th Corps were raised.

This latter division was nearly wiped out by the first rush of the Bulgarians in the war of 1912. The Third Army Corps was at Bulair, that narrow and strongly defended isthmus which connects the Gallipoli peninsula with the mainland. One of the divisions of this Corps was extended between Bulair and Rodosta ; the other divisions were at Balak Hissar and Gallipoli. When the Allies made their first attack on the Dardanelles, its shores were defended by these two divisions only.* The Fourth Army Corps had its headquarters at Smyrna, and its divisions at Smyrna, Denzeli, and Burdur. Its first task on mobilisation was to be the defence of the great seaport of Smyrna, the Liverpool of the Levant. It could be completely shifted by rail to the southern shores of the Dardanelles in three days ; to Constantinople in four days, and to Damascus in six days. The Fifth Army Corps was at Angora, the eastern terminus of the branch railway which takes off from the Anatolian Railway at Eski-Shehir. Its divisions were at Angora, Kastamuni, and Yuzgat. On mobilisation it could be concentrated and transported by rail to Constantinople in three days.

These five Corps formed what was officially called the First Group, for defence or attack on the European front. They were under one Inspector-General ; a German, Von Saunders ; and they formed the First Military District. They were well drilled, well clad, well shod, and well supplied with ammunition. They formed an excellent army, which could concentrate at any given point in the First Military District within four days.

The Sixth Army Corps had its headquarters at Aleppo, and its divisions at Aleppo, Baiburt, and Adana. Aleppo is connected by rail with Damascus. Adana is on the Baghdad Railway, and is also connected by rail with the small seaport of Mersina, forty miles away. It is well to note here that *this little stretch of a single track railway represents all the concessions which England asked for, or got, from Turkey, during the thirty years from the time of the Crimean War to the year* 1886. After the Crimean War, England could have got any concessions she desired all over the Turkish Empire ; but this little railway was all she asked for, and that for commercial purposes only. On the other hand, in less than five years after Germany had established her influence at Constantinople, the Germans had demanded and obtained concessions to the extent of two thousand miles of railway, and induced the impoverished Turkish Government to guarantee these railways at the rate of 17,000 francs per kilometre, annually.

The Seventh Army Corps, consisting of the 19th, 20th, 21st and 22nd Divisions, was distributed in Southern Syria and along the

---

*The *Tannine* (leading newspaper in Constantinople) and *Militär Wochenblatt* (Berlin) ; October, 1914.

eastern coast of the Red Sea. The Eighth Army Corps was much larger than any of the other Corps, and its headquarters were at Damascus. It consisted of five divisions; three of which were in Damascus itself, one between Damascus and Aleppo, and one, the 27th, at Haifa. The eight divisions from Damascus and Aleppo, together with what could be spared of the Seventh Corps, in Southern Syria, were to form an army of about 350,000 strong, for an attack on the Suez Canal and the invasion of Egypt. They would make use of the Hedjaz railway, to concentrate within 150 miles of the Suez Canal.

The Sixth, Seventh and Eighth Corps formed the Second Military District. The Inspector-General was Djemal Pasha, a Turk, of Arab extraction, and an able soldier. The Ninth Army Corps was at Erzeroum, the Tenth, at Erzinjan, and the Eleventh at Van. These three Corps formed the Third Military District.

The headquarters of the Twelfth Army Corps were at Mosul (about 230 miles, as the crow flies, north-by-west of Baghdad), one of its divisions being at Mosul, and the other at Kerkuk (90 miles south-east from Mosul, near the Persian frontier).

The Thirteenth Army Corps had its headquarters at Baghdad; one of its divisions being at Baghdad itself, and the other division, the 38th, at Basra.

Taking a general glance (with the assistance of a good map) at this strategic distribution of the military strength of the Ottoman Empire, we see that fifteen divisions were available for operations in Europe, twelve for the offensive against Egypt, and eleven for the Russo-Persian frontier and Mesopotamia.

In addition to the thirty-eight divisions of the Regular Army, Turkey had more than 200,000 irregular troops. German and Austrian newspapers said that she had half a million of such troops; but this is a highly exaggerated estimate. The irregulars consisted of Kurds from Armenia, and mongrel Arabs from the nomad tribes, between the Syrian and Persian frontiers.

There is no human being in the world more loathsome, more filthy, or more brutal than a Kurd. If a Kurd is half a mile on the windward side of you, you feel the whiff of a rag and bone shop on fire. The mongrel Arab is not much better. But *he* lives in the open, and takes off his clothes sometimes, which the Kurd never does. More than twenty years ago I travelled on the Turkish boat *Hamidyeh*, from Basra to Baghdad, with the officers and men of a brigade of Turkish infantry. When we got to Kut, a couple of hundred Kurds, with the effluvia of a herd of camels, came on board. But the Turkish soldiers rose in a body and pitched the Kurds out on to two barges which we were tugging up stream.

The Turkish officers enjoyed it immensely ; three of the Kurds died of wounds, and were pitched into the river before we got to Baghdad.

It is essential for the student to bear in mind the facts that I have mentioned about the organisation and distribution of the Turkish Army, so that he may more easily and clearly follow the events of the Great War as far as Turkey was concerned. During the months of August, September and October, 1914, the Germans in Turkey were working hard at their nefarious plots, and they succeeded completely in throwing dust into the eyes of the British and French representatives at Constantinople. It seems that these, especially the British, did not even go to the trouble of learning the Turkish language—the easiest language of Europe—while the German diplomats knew Turkish as well as the Turks themselves.

The *Goeben* and *Breslau,* two German warships which our Fleet had missed in the Mediterranean, came into Turkish waters, remained under German control in the Bosphorus, and a large German element was introduced into the Turkish fleet. German merchant vessels in Turkish waters were used as naval auxiliaries ; and their wireless apparatus was adapted to suit the communications with the German General Staff. Directly the Army was mobilised, large quantities of war material were sent to Damascus and Baghdad.

The German managers of affairs in Turkey employed all means, fair and foul, which might help to defeat England. A number of Turks, Arabs and Persians, who had been educated at German Universities, were detailed to go out and preach a Holy War, or *Jehad,* in Eastern Turkey, Persia, Afghanistan, Egypt and the Sudan. These missionaries proclaimed that the Kaiser had become a convert to Islam, and they promised that the Khalif (the Sultan of Turkey) would very soon announce a Jehad against the infidel. Lying stories were glibly told of the readiness and desire of the Mussulman subjects of England, France and Russia, to rise up at this summons ; and preparations were made for the manufacture of Indian Military uniforms at Aleppo, to give visible proof to the Syrian Arabs that the Indian Mussulmans were on their side. Egypt, which had been for a long time the poaching-ground of German missionaries and propaganda, was now considered ripe for revolt ; and the Khedive was at heart a sullen and treacherous enemy to English rule. Still, at the same time, the members of the Turkish Government were by no means united in their Councils. The Sultan himself very much objected to an open breach of neutrality ; and there is reason to believe that he honestly did his best to prevent such a calamity. The Grand

Vizier was a man of weak character ; but he showed his abhorrence
of war as strongly as his nature permitted. Djavid Bey, the
Finance Minister, warned the swash-buckling party that the
treasury was empty, and that he did not know where to turn to
raise a thousand pounds. The long-suffering Turkish people were
beginning to get tired of the new regime, the " Union and Progress "
rogues ; and many of them well knew that France and England
had been the best friends of Turkey in the past. But the Turkish
people were not allowed to have the smallest voice in the matter.
The Turkish administration was as completely in the hands of the
Army Chiefs as the Long Parliament, in our own History, had been
in the hands of Oliver Cromwell. In this case, the Turkish Cromwell,
Enver Pasha, was simply a puppet in the hands of his German
patrons and paymasters. The Turkish people had been unhappy
and oppressed under old Abd-ul-Hamid ; but now they found that
where he had chastised them with whips their present taskmasters
chastised them with scorpions, and Enver's little finger was thicker
than Abdul's loins. The much-vaunted "Committee of Union of
Progress " were united only in the idea of filling their own pockets
by fleecing the people, and their progress was only that of the
Rake, to national suicide.

This precious Committee began by doing the very things
they should never have attempted to do. The strength of Turkey
had always consisted in her religion and her peasantry. With the
Turk, religion takes the place of patriotism ; for a hundred genera-
tions has not yet expelled from his nature the nomadic spirit which
his Seljuk ancestors brought from Central Asia. A wise government
which desires a strong Turkish Empire should therefore encourage
in every way the national religion, and treat the peasantry with
that noble justice, tact, and kindness which Kitchener practised
towards the Egyptian fellaheen. But the " Young Turks " and
the " Committee of Union and Progress " sneered openly at, and
spoke with contempt of, the faith and doctrines of Islam. With
their German friends they showed themselves publicly at feasts
and banquets, where they ate pig's flesh, and got beastly drunk
on whisky, brandy and wine. They increased the already crushing
taxation of the peasantry ; they sold justice ; they proved far more
corrupt, more unscrupulous, and more brutal than their predecessors.

They were not all bad. Among their number were two very
able, honest and patriotic Turkish gentlemen : Nazim Pasha, and
Mohammed Shefket Pasha. These were self-respecting enough to
keep away from the public gorgings and swillings ; they resisted
with all their might the German influence in Turkish administration ;
and, worst of all, they were suspected of cherishing a secret friendship for, and admiration of England. They were both cruelly and
treacherously assassinated. When Enver had removed them out

of his way, he thought that the time to strike had now come. Acting on the advice of his German friends, he sent three Turkish torpedo boats to raid the large Russian seaport of Odessa. These sank and damaged several ships in the harbour, and bombarded the town. This took place on the 29th of October, 1914 ; and Sir L. Mallet, the English Minister, left Constantinople, on the first of November.

For the first time in History, the whole British Empire was at war with the Ottoman Empire.

The Turkish Soldier.

The Turkish infantry soldier had for many years a high reputation, especially when fighting on the defensive. Under Omar Pasha, in 1853, and under Osman Pasha, at Plevna, in 1877, he confirmed this reputation. His physique is good, his limbs sturdy, his nerves steady, and his powers of endurance almost incredible.

But in the Balkan War of 1912, his reputation, as a fighting man, fell very low. To account for this there are very natural and satisfactory reasons. He was badly led, and was not sufficiently trained and accustomed to his new armament ; his transport and supply department broke down ; he had no confidence in his commanders, and his commanders had no trust in him.

Here now, we come face to face with curious and interesting problems, well worth the best attention of all students of military history. In comparatively recent times, the ragged, bare-footed, half-starved, and badly-drilled Turkish soldiers had fought with brilliant success under men who were born military geniuses : Omar Pasha, Osman Pasha, Baker Pasha (an Englishman), and Mohammed Ali Pasha (a German by birth). And this was because they were then inspired by a strong, though simple, trust in their leaders ; and they firmly believed that they were fighting for their religion, their Khalif and their Padishah. But by 1912, an un-natural attempt had been made to overspread these sentiments and traditions with the soul-crushing and materialistic mechanical perfection of the German system.

The best trained soldier, in any army, is he in whom the Natural Forces are not crushed out of existence by the Acquired Forces. In the German system, Moral Force and the Natural Forces inherent in the man are never taken into account. The Turk was never meant, by his nature, to be a soldier of the German type ; the seeds sown by Von der Goltz and his brother officers fell on the thorny Natural Forces which sprang up and choked them. German efforts and endeavour certainly produced a machine, beautifully polished, like their " shining armour " ; but without any driving power, as it was lacking in steam. Every army has an individuality of its own ; and the Turkish Army is no exception to this rule. The Turkish soldier has been always at his best, as a soldier, when he feels that he is fighting for Islam and his Padishah ; but we cannot blame him if he fails to raise the steam of enthusiasm for those who treated Islam with open contempt ; for the gluttons and drunkards who now ruled the Army of the Faithful. His old Padishah, Abdul Hamid, who, with all his faults, had been a good Mussulman, was now hidden away, like a criminal, in a living tomb. The new Sultan was no more than an animated toy, a marionette worked by strings pulled in Berlin. Why shed his blood or risk life and limb for such a Padishah ? Why should he have any confidence in men who had already led him to defeat and disgrace ?

A perfect machine is a very fine thing, but an imperfect machine is only so much scrap iron. The Turkish soldier was now no longer a Turk, but a sort of military hybrid ; a mule without the kicking power of the beast, a rifle without the breech block. And so it is certain to become in every army in which the Natural Forces of the soldier are smothered and crushed out of him, by any mechanical and soulless system, such as that which has been for years so slavishly admired and copied by our own Brodericks and Haldanes.

Chapter III.

THE PART TO BE PLAYED BY TURKEY IN THE GERMAN IDEA OF THE STRATEGY OF THE GREAT WAR.

The chief interest of the Germans in the Turkish Army lay in Europe. They had impressed upon Turkish military commanders and statesmen the idea that Germany and Austria were absolutely certain to be victorious. Germany promised to restore to Turkey the lost Province of Thrace, and to give her also the fine harbour of Salonika, in case Greece did not declare for the Central Powers. Turkey was confidently informed that she should have nothing to fear from Greece or Bulgaria. Therefore, she would have no occasion to trouble herself about any fighting in her European Districts.

So now what Turkey had to think about was the best use she could make of the fifteen divisions—about 200,000 strong—which she had no need to employ in European warfare. The German commanders soon solved this problem for her. A cut-and-dried Plan of Campaign, worked out to the smallest detail, as far as could be foreseen, was sent from Berlin to Constantinople. With an army of about half a million of men, Turkey was to attack Russia in Trans-Caucasia, that is, in the direction of Erzeroum. Such an offensive was exactly what suited the plans of Germany just now. Russia was running short of ammunition, equipment and supplies, in Poland. A sudden, heavy stroke at her frontier between the Black and Caspian Seas, would draw away troops from that dangerously thinning line, a thousand miles long, which she was trying to hold between the Niemen and the Dniester. Again, the moving of a large Turkish Army to the east of Asia Minor would be sure to increase the trouble, long brewing and now coming to a head, in Persia ; whence the flames, fanned from the west, might haply extend to Afghanistan, Baluchistan, and India. But the most favourable opportunity for creating trouble towards India were in the German schemes, which were now ripe, on the shores of the Persian Gulf. For some years German agents had been very busy in these parts, on the Tigris, and in western Persia. Turks and Persians who had been educated in Germany, young men of great cunning and energy, were to be found at the court of Kabul, and among the turbulent tribes from Chitral to Chaman.

The Germans in Turkey never expected that Russia would assume the offensive in Armenia. They believed that she would have contented herself by merely standing on the defensive; which would allow a large Turkish force to push on into Persia, having left a containing force in front of the Russians. Enver Pasha and his German colleagues did think of the Dardanelles; but they rightly judged that the penetration of this difficult passage, defended by Krupp's heavy guns, would prove impossible.

The Persian Gulf is the scene of one of England's oldest enterprises in the Middle East. It had already been visited by English traders in the reign of Queen Elizabeth. In the reign of Charles II. they had established a large and flourishing trade at Bandar Abbas; and, off and on, for one hundred and fifty years, they had fought against the Dutch and Portuguese traders who had been trying to drive them from the Gulf. The first survey of the Persian Gulf was carried out by the Indian Navy; and for fifty years English seamen hunted down the Gulf pirates; at last succeeding in clearing them out of their dens along that rocky rugged shore of Arabia which still bears the name of the Pirate Coast.

Later on, England defended Persia against those who would have deprived her of her sea-board; England suppressed slavery and the gun-running in the Gulf; she wrestled with the plague, established hospitals, marked out the routes with buoys, encouraged peaceful trading, and vastly improved the condition of the people on the adjacent coasts. For three hundred years England, single-handed, carried out this beneficient work; yet she claimed no monopoly in the Gulf trade, nor did she ever once demand or beg one pennyworth of concessions. There is no nation in the world, and there has never been one in the history of the world, which can point to such a noble record of unselfish effort as England can show in the Persian Gulf.

It would certainly have been better for England and for humanity if she had not been quite so altruistic; for the work cost her many lives and much money, and the Arab, Turk and Persian know nothing of gratitude.

For our own protection, however, there is one thing we insisted on; namely, that no other Power should be allowed to seize and possess any territory in the Gulf, and no other flag should ever dominate its waters. This was necessary, to secure the safety of India; and the sea-approach to the Gulf is now barred by the strong naval strategic triangle of Aden, Karachi, and Bombay.

Mesopotamia was to be for Germany what Egypt was to England, and Morocco to France. Aye, and still more; it was to be the jumping-off place for plunges of conquest to the East, far beyond the dreams of Alexander the Great, or Napoleon. German professors lectured to excited audiences, telling them that in former times this blessed land of Mesopotamia could boast of cities far larger and wealthier than Berlin or Vienna ; that it supported a population of twenty millions, and that as it was in the past so it would be again.

If Germany could get a footing on the Gulf, not only would she have the monopoly of exploiting Mesopotamia, but she would also have considerably weakened the British hold on India. Her leading suit was the Baghdad Railway.

On the northern shores of the Persian Gulf there is a fairly good harbour, called Koweit, or Grane. About the time of the Russo-Japanese War (1905), some Germans were appointed Agents of the Hamburg-Amerika Line, and got concessions from the Turkish Government for some large tracks of land by the shores of the Gulf, at Koweit. The local Arab sheikhs protested that the Turkish Government had no power to grant these concessions ; and they appealed to the British Government. Turkey then sent a small body of soldiers from Basra to Koweit, to protect the " peaceful German traders " from the Arabs. The land which had been conceded to these traders was already being surveyed and prepared to be made the terminus of the Baghdad Railway on the Persian Gulf.

For the previous century British influence and interests were supreme from Baghdad to the Persian Gulf. Further, this was the only part of the whole world in which English commerce had succeeded in holding off the German trader, with his Government subsidies and his strong political backing.

Shortly after the Crimean War (1856) England engaged in a War with Persia, and landed troops at Bushire. Since then Persia has given no trouble. For years before the Great War, a line of British steamers went regularly up the Tigris to Baghdad, which is the centre of the caravan trade between Persia and Turkey. In 1912, the foreign trade of Baghdad amounted to five million pounds sterling, of which four and a half millions were British and British India trade. The goods exported from Germany to Baghdad, in the same year, were of the value of £80,000.

About the beginning of the present century, a large irrigation scheme was drawn up under the direction of Sir William Willcocks, the object of which was to render fruitful the wide plains about the site of ancient Babylon. The scheme was to cost £22,000,000. This would have been the expense of reclaiming and getting under cultivation three million acres of some of the most fertile land in the world. England was ready to produce every penny of this money, at a moderate rate of interest ; but English business men naturally wanted better security for their investments than the mere promises of the " Young Turks." Germany had her hands full with the Baghdad Railway ; France was lending all her spare cash to Russia ; and so the irrigation scheme fell through.

Then came another factor, still more important in the commerce of the British Empire. The British Government had invested three millions sterling in acquiring control over the Anglo-Persian Oil Fields, the principal source of supply of oil fuel for the British Navy. Other sources of our oil supply, in Burmah, the Punjab (near the Indus at Attock), in Egypt, convenient to the Suez Canal, have escaped the greedy maw of the American Oil Trust ; and we should fight tooth and nail to keep them in our own hands. The Anglo-Persian Oil Fields are comparatively close to the Eastern Turkish frontier ; and the oil is conveyed from the works at Ahwaz, in pipes, laid by the side of the Karun River, down to Mohammerah. The native tribes in the neighbourhood were paid to protect the pipe-line, or, rather, to leave it alone.

In 1907, England and Russia came to an agreement with regard to their respective policies in Persia. The gist of the arrange-ment was that Northern Persia should be Russia's " Sphere of Influence," while the Eastern part of Southern Persia should be England's. Both Russia and England recognised that a great military power like Germany, permanently established at Baghdad, not having come there for the good of her health only, but aggres-sively and truculently, would prove very dangerous to their interests. The two great Powers in the Entente were not in 1907 such good friends as they were in 1914 ; and some of the old suspicions were still clinging to them both. So in order that neither of them could filch an advantage over the other, they decided that the Persian Police, or gendarmerie, in number about 6,000, should be officered by neutrals. Unfortunately for England, they decided to have Swedish Officers for the gendarmerie ; and later on it was found that many of these same Swedish officers were in German pay, and were busy in German propaganda.* Neither England nor Russia desired that Persia should be dragged into the War. But the German ambassador in Persia held different views. By liberal distribution of *backsheesh* he got the gendarmes on his side, with various bands of highway robbers and cut-throats ; and he succeeded in raising a rebellion in the Russian sphere of influence. The Turkish and German newspapers tried to dignify the doings of these

---

*There is no use in anybody attempting to deny this. The author has documentary evidence, containing the names of some of the officers, and the moneys paid to them by Prince Reuss and Von Harting.

20

bribed ragamuffins* by announcing the rebellion as the outbreak of the Holy War (Jehad) in the Middle East. But there was nothing holy about it ; religion had nothing whatever to do with such a ruffianly plot as that to murder the European residents in Bushire. Some straggling bodies of Turkish irregulars, from the Mosul garrison, entered Persia, and they announced far and wide that they were the Advanced Guard of an Army which was going to conquer India, while their brothers were conquering Egypt. The Germans fanned the rebellion by publishing newspapers in Persia, with articles written and printed in German, French and Persian.

The geographical position of the eastern part of Turkey is such that all the most direct trade routes from Asia to Europe passed through these parts and converged towards Europe on Constantinople. For many centuries this great and ancient city was the centre of the commercial world, the clearing-house for the merchandise of Europe, Asia, and Africa. From Scutari, on the Asiatic side of the Bosphorus, the great trade routes of the world run right across Asia Minor to Aleppo, southwards, and Baghdad, eastwards. At Aleppo the signpost towards India pointed down the Euphrates Valley, and on to Basra. The signpost to Egypt pointed down by the Syrian coast road and across the Sinai Desert. Between the Indian road and the Egyptian Road lies the great Syrian Desert. On the way from Constantinople to Syria, as you get near Aleppo, there are two parallel ranges of mountains, the Taurus and the Amanus, which converge towards the sea at the Gulf of Alexandretta. In the lower elevations of these mountains there is a pass by which many armies have moved into Syria from the north-west. It is called the Cilician Gates. In the Great War this celebrated pass was of the highest strategic importance to the Turks and to the Allies. Any army moving from Asia Minor, with Egypt as an objective ; any army moving from Mesopotamia into Asia Minor, must pass through it. Thus the two doors into Turkey from the East, are Erzeroum in the north, and the Cilician Gates on the south.

From the mountain valleys south-west of Erzeroum a number of streams converge to form the great river Tigris, which runs down to the Persian Gulf ; its course being roughly parallel to the boundary between Turkey and Persia. The most important place on the banks of this river is the ancient and classical city of Baghdad, the former capital of the powerful Caliphs of Islam "in the golden prime of good Haroun al Rashid."

*When I was at Ahwaz, in 1904, I wanted to go up through Shuster to Ispahan and Teheran ; but the Consul at Ahwaz put me off, with his blood-curdling stories of the Bakhtiari cut-throats and the lions.

There is nowhere in the world a scene more beautiful than the Tigris, just below Baghdad, at daybreak. You wake up in the land of Omar Khayyam, of the stately minarets and golden domes, the graceful date palms, the bowers of roses, the Persian wheel at the old well, the liquid notes of the nightingales in the orange groves :

> And lo the hunter of the East has caught
> The Sultan's turret in a blaze of light.

Baghdad is the most important city between Constantinople and Delhi ; between the Mediterranean Sea and the Indian Ocean. It is about 1,200 miles from Constantinople, as the crow flies ; but the railway with its curves and turnings will be about 1,600 miles. It is nearly equally distant from the Caspian Sea and the Persian Gulf, about 400 miles. It is 700 miles from the Black Sea on the north, 600 miles from the Suez Canal on the west, and 400 miles from Teheran, the capital of Persia. It occupies both banks of the Tigris, but the greater part of the city lies on the eastern or left bank. The two parts are connected by a bridge of boats (1915). A tottering old brick wall surrounded the city on the eastern side ; and the neighbouring country is so flat and so devoid of any naturally strong positions that a successful defence could only be attempted some twelve miles or more from the city itself. Against an attack from the south the best position of defence is indicated by the line of the unfordable river Diyalah.

During some years before the Great War the importance of Baghdad was considerably enhanced by the extension of the Baghdad Railway and its branches ; from Constantinople to the Egyptian frontier, in one direction, and to the Persian frontier in the other. This latter section crossed the Euphrates at Djerablis.

Particular attention is requested to the following facts in connection with the construction of this Railway. If you look at the map, you will see that the shortest and most direct route from Aleppo to Baghdad would not at all follow the track of the Railway as laid down by German strategists. If the Baghdad Railway had been built for *commercial* purposes only, it would have run from Aleppo *not* north-east, but south-east ; along the right bank of the Euphrates, crossing this river conveniently, thirty miles west of Baghdad. Now what could have been the reason for constructing it longer and more expensive, four hundred miles out of its way, through the bleak and barren regions of northern Mesopotamia, and down the right bank of the Tigris, when it would have been much easier, cheaper, and more convenient, to follow the direct route along the old caravan road by the Euphrates, through a comparatively fertile country, down to the Persian Gulf ? To this there is a very clear and correct answer. The railway was laid down in this round-about way, first of all, because the Germans were guaranteed about £700 sterling, yearly, for every mile of railway they built. But there is a still stronger reason ; a military and political one. The railway running along the western bank of the Tigris for four hundred miles (*i.e.*, from Mosul to Basra), facing the Persian frontier the whole way, was to be a strategic railway, at any point of which a large force might be easily and quickly concentrated, for the penetration—peaceful or otherwise—of Western Persia, and for driving a Turco-German wedge in between the English and Russian spheres of influence.

The section from Aleppo to Mosul was surveyed in 1909 ; and shortly before the Great War broke out, its construction was being pushed on vigorously towards the east. In April, 1915, construction trains were drawing near Mosul, on a roughly-laid track and rails. At this time the representative of the American Press in Constantinople went to the railway terminus near the Bosphorus shore, to see, as he expected, German soldiers, and guns and ammunition coming into Turkey. But he saw nothing of the sort. For five days and nights, he tells us, trains rolled into the station, three trains an hour, piled up with rails and sleepers and pontoon boats ; railway plant and material for laying tracks, building bridges, and crossing rivers. There was to be no lack of labour in Asia Minor. Thousands of Armenians were said to have been massacred who had never been massacred at all ; they had been taken away from their native country, and organized in regiments of navvies ; eighty-five thousand of them were working on the Baghdad Railway. These wretched Armenians, ill-fed, ragged, driven by the lash, dragged from their untilled fields, torn from their homes in which the trembling women and children were left exposed to massacre or worse, perished from starvation and cruelty in the sands of Northern Mesopotamia.

Germany had bluffed both England and Russia into compliance with her next move, of two branch railways ; one to go eastwards from Mosul to the Persian frontier at the little town of Sulemaniyeh, the other from Baghdad to the frontier town of Khanikin. These would carry the Baghdad Railway right on to the Persian frontier, and place in German hands the principal meeting points of all the caravan routes and natural trade routes in Western Persia.

The next point at which Germany aimed was evidently Hamadan ; because from here the main caravan route runs straight across to Kerman, by Yezd, and then to Baluchistan, Afghanistan and British India.

There are other points in this Turco-Persian frontier from which Persia could be easily entered by an army based on Baghdad ; that is, *if the ultimate object of that Army was merely to occupy*

Persia and go no further. But if an Army entered Persia from the west, *with the ultimate object of pushing on to Quetta,* then the line of operation from the Baghdad direction would be the safest and best ; especially being secure against a flank attack, by a sea-power, coming from the direction of the Persian Gulf.

Some of our Politicians, whose scanty knowledge of historical and geographical facts does but small credit even to their secondary education, have said and have written that the march of an Army from Baghdad, across Persia and Baluchistan, to the Indus, may be dismissed as a physical impossibility. But would these politicians, at the beginning of the present century, have believed that Turkish Troops, commanded by German Officers, fifteen hundred miles from Constantinople, and two thousand miles away from the ultimate base in Germany, would be able to defeat forces which had every opportunity and full leisure to concentrate and meet them on the banks of the Tigris ? From Constantinople to Baghdad is just about the same distance as from Baghdad to Quetta ; and the natural difficulties of the former distance are much greater than those of the latter.

The great Swedish traveller, Dr. Sven Hedin, wrote a book, "Overland to India," which was published shortly before the Great War. Why should this explorer select the long and devious way by Teheran, Kerman and Baluchistan, if he only wanted to get to Quetta ? By simply landing at Karachi, he could have got from here to Quetta in ten hours by rail. But this would not have suited his game. In the early part of the Great War he was received as an honoured guest at Imperial Headquarters ; he was a sort of Court Historian at the Great Russian defeat of 1915 ; he attended the German Councils of War at Constantinople, and the head of the Gendarmerie in Persia was a personal friend of his. The fact is that Dr. Sven Hedin selected for his exploration the route by which India was to be invaded, and may still be invaded, by land. The more northern route by Kabul, was the one selected by Alexander the Great ; and returning from India, the Great Conqueror chose the route along the coast of Baluchistan and the Persian Gulf. But this latter route is now barred by England's Command of the Sea ; so that Sven Hedin struck the best and safest route, between the northern and southern routes. Anybody who reads his book can see that it is a very useful guide for the march of a body of troops ; a military report of a road reconnaissance sent in by a very capable staff officer. Here you get where there is plenty of water ; there you get firewood ; over yonder any amount of grass and grain to be had. He says : " Why do not Englishmen travel in motor-cars over this trade route ? They could drive from Seistan to Nushki (near Quetta) in a few days." He foresaw how mechanical transport was to increase the mobility of armies.

But to run your mechanical transport successfully you must have plenty of petrol. No difficulty whatever. At the beginning of the Eastern Turkish Campaign, against Russia to the north, and England to the south, the objectives were the *Russian sources of oil supply at Batoum and Baku*, and *the British Oil Fields at Ahwaz*. If they could only have got hold of these oil supplies, the motor transport would have followed at once. Motor cars were already running between Aleppo and Baghdad, and there was nothing whatever to prevent them from running across Persia by Sven Hedin's route. Alexander the Great led an army of 100,000 men by this way twenty-three centuries ago ; the great Arab Commander, Mohammed ben Kassim, led 50,000 men from Basra to Karachi, in the eighth century ; and Nadir Shah, in the eighteenth century, at the head of 120,000 men, marched from Kerman to India, and captured Delhi. About fifty years ago a British Officer, Major Ewan Smith, who was said to know every square yard of land in Persia and Baluchistan, wrote : " The Persians, should they think fit, could easily march a large army across Baluchistan, in the direction of, and up to, the Sind frontier, without any material obstacle, finding provisions and water the whole way." Now if a Persian army could, in the opinion of an experienced British Officer, carry out a successful march to India, forty years ago, it is in no way fantastic that the German General Staff should think it possible for a Turco-German Army, well provided with mechanical transport, to cover the same ground in less time, and with greater chances of success.

Chapter IV.

STUDY OF THE MESOPOTAMIAN CAMPAIGN.

The serious and conscientious military student must not imagine for a moment that the practical knowledge of a campaign, for the soldier and the strategist, is by any means confined to knowing by rote the names of the places where battles were fought, and the dates on which they were fought. Strategy demands rather the exercise of a man's thinking and reasoning powers than the useless burdening of his memory.

At all the important turning points of the campaign, the student should give himself the following important question, and solve it to the best of his ability.

Appreciate the situation, and comment on the action taken by General " X," or General " Y," Commanders of the opposing forces.

Imagine yourself in the place of General " X " or " Y," as the case may be ; then give—

(1) A clear and concise statement of the object in view, or *the task to be done.*

(In doing this, be careful to avoid diffuseness, obscurity, and any remarks which have no bearing on the point.)

(2) The situation, distribution and strength of *your own force.*

(3) The situation, distribution and strength of *the enemy.*

(4) The courses open to you.

(5) The courses open to the enemy.

In giving (2) and (4) you should compare the relative strength of yourself and the enemy. You should take into account the *moral* on both sides. For instance, if the enemy has been badly beaten a day or two before, he is probably demoralised, and not likely to assume the offensive. If he has not been beaten, if there has been a drawn battle, if he has just received reinforcements, he may assume the offensive. Mark the influence of politics on the course of events ; as General LEE did during the first three years of the American Civil War ; as NAPOLEON did at the opening of the Campaign of 1815 ; as Japan did at the close of the Manchurian Campaign ; and as FOCH did in 1918.

A rough sketch, showing the general topography of the theatre of operations, the communications, and the decisive strategic points, will help to make the situation clear.

With regard to positions, point out what advantages they offer to the enemy; also their disadvantages.

Describe the lines of communication; their nature, and security.

Point out how you are going to manage about your supply and transport.

Take into account the climatic conditions in the theatre of operations.

In (3) and (5) the courses open to yourself, and the courses open to the enemy:

Give clearly the possibilities of the different courses of action, as far as they can be foreseen.

Always give the enemy credit for acting soundly, and making no mistakes.

Is he likely to take the initiative, and assume the offensive?

What action on his part would be likely to interfere most effectively with your plans?

What counter measures would you take?

What is known of the opposing commander?

If the enemy remains where he is, how and where are you going to attack him?

If he retires, when can you come up with him?

If he advances, where is the best place for you to meet him?

What time is available, and what preparations are advisable?

Are your flanks secure?

Having considered all these points, decide whether you can at once proceed to the attainment of the object in view (1); if not, settle as to what action on your part will most effectively assist your own side and interfere with probable plans of the enemy.

And, finally:

    (6) Conclude by stating your proposed line of action, giving a short summary of the reasons which led to it.

Other important questions which the student should put to himself in the course of the campaign are:—

    (1) Why was the course adopted by.....................on.....................right (or wrong)?

    (2) Suggest any other course that he might have adopted.

    (3) Discuss the plan of operation, method of carrying it out, and effects produced.

    (4) Describe briefly, with aid of hand sketch, the battle of " X."

(5) What were the salient points in the battle of " X " ? Describe them briefly.

(6) Discuss the disposition of the contending forces in the battle of " X." Point out any errors that were made.

(7) Give the tactical lessons to be learnt from the battle of " X."

(8) Discuss the topography of the theatre of operations in the campaign of..

(9) State fully the sequence of events from (some important date) to (some other date).
> (an approach to, or retreat from some important position to another).

(10) Show the influence that natural obstacles (or *politics* or *sea-power*) had on the strategy of this campaign.

(11) What were the errors (or causes) which led to (som e particular) result ?

The student would do well to jot down, first of all the headings of each paragraph in his answer, in pencil, and see that the events referred to are placed in their proper order.

Before entering into the actual events of the campaign, it is necessary to deal with the topography of this theatre of operations.

The Oil Fields are in Persian territory ; well within the Persian border. The most direct way of getting to them is from the Port of Mohammerah, where the Karun—the only river in Persia— joins the Shatt ul Arab, the river which is formed by the combined waters of the Tigris and Euphrates, after uniting at a place called Kurna. This river—the Shatt ul Arab—was entirely in Turkish territory. Entering it from the Persian Gulf, you have the little fort and cable station of Fao on your left ; then you go northward to Basra, on the western bank, twenty-five miles above Mohammerah. Between Fao and Basra on the same bank, and nearly opposite to the junction of the Karun with the Shatt ul Arab, is Sahil, where one of the first small fights of the campaign took place.

The Karun river is navigable up to Ahwaz ; and the distance from Basra to Ahwaz, as the crow flies, it just on eighty miles. The country between these two places belongs to the Kab Arabs, who had never been unfriendly to the British.

The first idea of our political and military authorities seems to have been that if we occupied Basra, on the left, and Ahwaz on the right, of this eighty-mile line, the protection of the oil-fields would have been sufficiently secured. The oil refineries and stores were at Abadan, some twelve miles south-east of Mohammerah.

At a distance of 120 miles north-west of Ahwaz, and the same distance north of Basra, there was a strong position on the left, or eastern, bank of the Tigris, called Amarah ; and 120 miles up the river from Amarah, a place called Kut. From Amarah as a base, an attack could be easily carried out against either Ahwaz or Basra. And also, 100 miles north-west of Basra, was the old Arab town of Nasiriyeh, on the river Euphrates. From Kurna, which marks the junction of the Tigris and Euphrates, to Fao, is 100 miles (following the course of the river) ; and Basra is nearly half-way between these two places. Amarah is 60 miles north of Kurna ; and if we take Amarah as the centre of a circle, with a line 120 miles as radius and look upon our circle as the disc of a clock, we shall have Ahwaz at 3.30, Basra at 5.30, Nasiriyeh at 7.30, and Kut at 10.30. From Kut to Baghdad is 100 miles ; and 25 miles south-by-east of Baghdad is Ctesiphon. A river called the Shatt-al-Hai connects Kut, on the Tigris, with Nasiriyeh on the Euphrates ; its length with its bendings, is about 100 miles.

Opening of the Campaign.

Although war was not declared by England against Turkey until the 5th of November, 1914, still British statesmen well knew, for some weeks before this, that Turkey was powerless to resist being pushed into the arena. The first thing to think about then was the security of the Persian oil fields. In the beginning of October, the 16th Brigade of the Poona Division, under the command of General Delamain, was with all secrecy sent up from Bombay to the head of the Persian Gulf. Delamain's orders were vague and indefinite* ; for, from the beginning to the end of this unfortunate campaign, those in authority rarely gave anything like definite and positive orders; but took care to frame them in such a way that if the result was a failure, the subordinate who had to carry out the orders could be proved to have been in the wrong.

Delamain was told to do what he could to protect the oil works at Abadan, and if possible, to occupy the port of Basra. He landed his force on Bahrein Island, where the pearl fisheries are, and where the drinking water is got from cool springs in the sea itself. For nearly a month Delamain did nothing, which showed his wisdom ; and at the end of the second week in November, General Sir Arthur Barrett arrived from Bombay with the rest of the Poona, or Sixth, Division. The British Force now at the head of the Persian Gulf was 15,000 strong ; but for some extra-

---

*Speaking of this opening phase of the Campaign, Sir W. Robertson, C.I.G.S., wrote (18-9-1916) : " I have been unable to find any clear instructions defining exactly the mission of Force D."

ordinary reason which has never come to light, it was entirely without transport, landing material, barges, or even rafts. Their objective, Basra, was thirty miles away ; and the enemy* was lying in wait for them, in a trackless jungle of date-palms and thick undergrowth. Just before War was declared, the Captains of a few ships in Basra harbour got wind of what was about to happen ; they slipped down the Shatt ul Arab, and entered the safe estuary of the Karun, near Mohammerah. They now came forward, and helped Barrett, by lending him their boats and the assistance of their crews ; without which he could not have landed his force.

The garrison of the small Turkish advanced post at Fao ran away after firing a few shots ; and joined their main body, at Sahil. This consisted of about 5,000 men, under the command of Subih Bey, Governor of Basra. On the 17th of November, Barrett struck them, holding them in front, and turning their right with his main attack. They fought well, and did not quit their position until more than a thousand of them were killed and wounded. Our casualties were nearly 600. The gallant Dorset Regiment particularly distinguished itself in this fight, carrying out two very successful charges with the bayonet. This action decided the fate of Basra.

It is possible that the comparative ease with which we won the battle of Sahil gave our commanders there the very false impression that the Turks were but poor fighting-men ; which may account for some serious mistakes and errors of judgment made later on in the campaign. In the open, the Turk cannot stand up against the British soldier, though he is superior to the Indian Sepoy ; but, behind earthworks there is no soldier in the world that can hold his own better than the Turk.

On the 23rd November, General Barrett ran up the Union Jack on the top of the finest and best built house in Basra, that which had been previously the residence of the German Consul.

Having now secured the covering positions of Basra, on the left, and Ahwaz, on the right of any hostile movement towards the Persian Gulf and the oil district, it was expected and hoped in high quarters, both in Delhi and London, that we should not go any further into Mesopotamia ; and General Barrett himself expressed his opinion that we should do well to hold and strengthen our position as we then stood. But we could scarcely do this with safety ; for we had now to face an unforeseen and difficult problem which demanded solution.

*33rd Division of the Turkish Army.

At a distance of 120 miles north-west of Ahwaz, and exactly the same distance north of Basra, there was a strong position on the left bank of the Tigris ; Amarah, held by a force of about 6,000 infantry under the command of Aziz Bey. From this place as a base, a strong Turkish force could easily make a dash for Ahwaz, while containing any force that might be sent against Amarah from Basra. We could not afford to ignore Amarah ; so we were compelled to go up the Tigris and capture it. If the German Chief Staff had been faced with this problem, they would have solved it by organizing a force to destroy Amarah ; and they would have done the job thoroughly ; they would not have left a stick or a stone or a human being or a blade of grass to show where Amarah had once stood. Hard and cruel, it may be said ; but it would have saved thousands of lives and millions of money, in the long run ; and *it was War.*

" Is it true," said Lucien Bonaparte to his brother Napoleon, " that you ordered the gunners to fire blank cartridge at the mob ? " " By no means," replied the god of War ; " that would have been a useless waste of life."

At this time the Commanders of the British Force were evidently under the impression that there was only one direction from which the enemy would be likely to launch an attack against Basra ; namely, from Amarah and down the Tigris. But they gradually began to learn something about the military geography of the country in which they were fighting.

The Shatt el Hai runs down from Kut, on the Tigris, to Nasiriyeh on the Euphrates. About sixteen miles before this river reaches the Euphrates, it breaks up into two or three branches, running through filthy and stagnant, reedy swamps, which stretch to within twelve miles west of Basra. While Barrett's eyes and thoughts were turned towards Amarah, the wily Turk was quietly concentrating a force at Nasiriyeh, using the water-ways of the Shatt el Hai and the Euphrates, while making ostentatious preparations for a desperate defence of Kurna.

Directly opposite Kurna, and on the eastern bank of the Tigris, is situated the village of Mezera, which the Turks had put into a state of defence ; and they thus commanded both banks of the Tigris. Kurna is about forty miles north of Basra ; and when Barrett had gone up and looked at its rough defences through his field-glasses, he smiled at them with an expression of contempt. He believed that a detachment of the Norfolk Regiment, with three gunboats, would be quite sufficient to take the defended Turkish positions of Kurna and Mezera. He was doomed to disappointment. The attack proved a failure ; though Colonel Fraser, who was in command, struck at the Turks with great vigour and bravery. It was only then that Barrett sent up a force, under General Fry, which proved equal to the task, and which successfully captured the positions, taking 1,200 prisoners of war and nine guns, on the 9th December, 1914.

Various Plans of Campaign.

In the beginning of January, 1915, the Mesopotamian Campaign was being very successfully fought out in the London Press, by Messrs. Lovat Fraser, Horatio Bottomley, and Hilaire Belloc. The various plans of these able and intelligent writers would have proved worthy of attention if only the writers had any practical knowledge of the conditions of fighting, or of the physical, geographical, or meteorological factors, which prevailed in Mesopotamia. Still, there was one interesting article, written by a retired officer of the Indian Army, who evidently knew the subject about which he expressed his opinion. He suggested that the positions in Mesopotamia, which we had gained up to that time, should be held on the defensive, by such of the Indian troops as were accustomed to hot climates, and by Sudanese regiments from Egypt. All British Troops in the Expeditionary " D " Force should be withdrawn, during the hot season, to the high and healthy plateaux of Western Persia ; and then come back at the beginning of the next cold weather, when the whole of the British Force would assume the offensive ; push on to Baghdad and Mosul, and join the Russians coming down from the North.

In the beginning of April, 1915, General Townshend, who had succeeded General Barrett in command of the Sixth Division, suggested a plan somewhat similar to the above, to General Sir John Nixon, just appointed Commander-in-Chief of the whole British Force in Mesopotamia. Townshend's plan was that General Gorringe, with the 12th Division, should move up the Karun to a convenient point north of Ahwaz ; make an entrenched camp there, and push forward a strong advanced post, say to Hawazeh, forty miles south-east of Amarah, to threaten the left flank of any Turkish advance down the Tigris to Basra, or to fall back, fighting, to Gorringe's entrenched camp covering Ahwaz. Nixon said it was a splendid idea, but——it would involve a violation of Persian territory.

These infernal " buts " always prevented Nixon from being a successful commander. At the big manœuvres of the Northern Army (India) which were held shortly before the Great War broke out, Nixon was in command of the invading " Blue "

Force, advancing from the Indus. There his " buts " lost him
nearly all his guns ; which were captured, on the move, by a
magnificent, well-timed, and dashing swoop of the Tenth Royal
Hussars. At the conference afterwards, when the Director of
Manœuvres (General Sir James Willcocks) asked him how he
managed to lose his guns, he replied : " But the Tenth Hussars
had no business to be there ! " His sensitiveness about the Persian
frontier, which was then being crossed, day and night, by Russians,
Turks, Kab Arabs and Bakhtiaris, though praiseworthy in a
country farmer, a game-keeper, or a custom-house officer, was
nothing short of deplorable in a General.

Mesopotamia as a Theatre of Military Operations.

The conditions of carrying out a campaign in Mesopotamia
were altogether different from those in any other theatre of operations in which our forces were engaged. The difficulties, physical
and climatic, to be overcome, were greater than any which had
ever been experienced by the British Army. In the wide, flat and
trackless deserts between the Persian frontier and Syria there is
no opportunity of outflanking or enveloping an enemy, so long as
he extends. Concentration is easier, except where there are
swamps and marshes ; and, as the terrain is flat, cavalry can be
well used in pursuit. Here there was not to be found, as in France
and Flanders, fixed lines of trenches, supported by impregnable
flanks. The Turks showed themselves very skilful in taking up
good positions, and digging themselves in ; but once their front was
broken they often ran, giving the cavalry a chance. Yet sometimes they clung to their trenches until they were driven out by
the bayonet.

The floods, from the rains, as a rule, begin about the end of
February. They form huge shallow lakes on both sides of the river;
which, later on, become putrid, evil-smelling, feverish swamps. Old
irrigation canals, many of them broad and deep, run out on both sides
of the river, and form great obstacles to transport. The heat is
terrific ; at sunrise it is sometimes 110° F., and in the afternoon as
much as 125°. The sands, baking during the day, retain their heat ;
so that the nights are sometimes as hot as the summer day in
India. There is absolutely no shade of any sort ; a blinding glare
is reflected from the yellowish-grey earth and steely water, and
there are no colours on which to rest the eye ; nothing but mad-
dening glare. The land is alive with vermin. In the cold weather
there is the plague of lice, and flies. With the warm weather
comes the flea, and flies. When the days get hotter, there are the mos-
quitoes, and flies ; with the cursed little sand-fly, from dark to dawn,
all the year round. The flies are not at all like English flies ; they are a
trifle larger, and more aggressive ; with a cold steely gloss on the back

and wings. When a man is dying they settle in bunches on his eyes ; and often before he is cold they have eaten his eyes out. If, in despair, you try to avoid all these fly pests by going out to sleep in the open, you run the risk of snakes, centipedes, and scorpions.

As for the people who wander about the country—for they cannot be said to dwell there—a very correct description of them is given by Sir Mark Sykes, who knew them well.

He says : " As for the population, it is base, semi-nomadic Arab ; cruel, treacherous and rascally ; yet predatory with the primitive Arab instinct. To these people, Turkish corruption, smugglers, and a year's war have brought a wealth of arms and ammunition. Without any cohesion or policy, they are neither for English or Turk. On the day of battle they haunt the outskirts of the fight, plunder the wounded and stragglers impartially, harass the retreat of the defeated side, hoist white flags over their tents, and make professions of unswerving fidelity to whomsoever happens to be in the ascendant."

They are fierce and fanatical ; splendid horsemen ; they hate the Turks with a deadly hatred, and look down with the greatest contempt on the Persians.

But *they speak Arabic* ; and it is as surprising to hear one of these untamable savages speak good classic Arabic as it would be to hear an English scavenger recite the *Canterbury Tales* of Chaucer. Now Mohammedans all over the world repeat their prayers in the Arabic of the Koran* ; and the only thing sacred to the Mohammedan Pathan or Punjabi is his prayers. Therefore it can be easily understood that when these Pathans and Punjabis were brought from India, to fight against and kill their brothers in religion, speaking the sacred language, they should hesitate to do so, and throw down their arms when ordered to go into action against the Arabs. It was, from the first, very injudicious to send Mohammedan soldiers from India to fight against Arabs and Turks in Mesopotamia.

The Battles of Shaiba and Nasiriyeh.

A gallant and capable Turkish Commander, Suleiman Askeri, who had been wounded by a shell at the battle of Kurna, had gone back quickly through Amarah ; and, handing over the defence of this place to Halim Bey and Aziz Bey, with special injunction to keep the English attracted in this direction, dashed up the river to Kut. Here he was met by a few battalions which had been sent down by Nureddin Pasha, the Turkish Commander-in-

---

*Just as Roman Catholics all over the world pray in Latin.

Chief of Baghdad. These he brought down south, by the Shatt el Hai, some of them by water, but the majority of them marching. He was followed by a mob of Kurds, amounting to about 3,000. When he reached Nasiriyeh, in the beginning of April, a great number of Arabs joined him. His total force was about 16,000 strong, with 18 mountain guns. His intention was to swoop down from the north-west on to Basra. But Barrett had heard of his movements, and interpreted them correctly. The English General looked round to select a good position of defence ; and he pitched on Shaiba, twelve miles west-by-north of Basra. Here he made a strongly entrenched camp ; and placed in it the 16th, 18th and 30th Brigades, under the command of General Mellis.

Shortly after daybreak on the 14th April the piquets and outposts of the British Force came tumbling over each other back into the trenches ; with Suleiman Askeri, leading his regular Turkish battalions, at their heels. Swarms of Arab horsemen appeared out of the morning mist, on their left flank ; while on the Turkish right the Kurds approached, yelping like jackals, with the malice of hell on their hideous faces, as they appeared to the British soldiers in the trenches. Suleiman was too optimistic : if *his* men had been in the trenches, and the British attacking, he might have stood some chance ; but, the other way round, the odds were a long way against him. The assailants of the entrenchments made no feints at various points ; they went straight headlong at the position, with reckless dash, and even penetrated the defence in some places. Certain Mohammedan companies in the position, shook, staggered, and broke ; but the backbone of the force was sound ; and, after some hours of very severe fighting, the Turks retreated, pursued by the victorious British, and by the greater part of the Arab horsemen who had been, only a few hours before, the sworn allies of the Turks. Suleiman, falling back fighting, saw his cowardly allies go on the side of his enemies. Rolling his dark bloodshot eyes in wrath, he roared out maledictions, in the name of the Prophet, on the treacherous sons of dogs who had so basely deserted him, when a bullet struck him full in the face, and he fell.* Then the Turkish retreat became a headlong rout ; the pursuit and slaughter went on till night fell.

The Turkish losses were 2,500 killed and wounded, and 800 prisoners. The British lost 20 officers killed, 40 wounded, and about 1,200 of the other ranks, killed and wounded.

General Mellis here established his reputation as commander of a defensive position ; and such was the wholesome respect

---

*It was reported that he had committed suicide ; but Hassan Bey, of the Turkish Artillery, in this battle, told the author that he saw Suleiman fall, as stated above.

instilled into the Turks by the gallant Norfolks, that in the whole subsequent course of the campaign, they never again attempted to carry British trenches. Shaiba was for them a severe and expensive lesson.

The victory at Shaiba relieved Basra of any further danger from the west ; but our line of operations from Basra and Kurna northwards would not be secure so long as a hostile force remained at Nasiriyeh. Therefore early in July (1915) an expeditionary force, to operate against this place, was organized under the command of General Gorringe, with the 12th Division, the 18th Brigade, and the field artillery of Townshend's (6th) Division.

There has never been such an extraordinary expedition in the whole history of the British Army. It can be correctly called an amphibious expedition, more suitable for crocodiles or swamp buffaloes than for human beings. The whole country between the two great rivers was flood where it was not marsh ; there was no way of knowing whether the water was two feet or twenty feet deep, as the beds of the old irrigation canals were not known, or marked. The force advanced, sometimes wading, sometimes in boats, and sometimes swimming. On they went, through the creeks and pools and slimy clay, in the date palm forest or under the merciless baking sun, tormented by thick swarms of loathsome insects, and sniped by the still more loathsome Arabs. Where a man fell, either by exhaustion or a stray bullet, there he was left ; and the crowds of vultures moving overhead marked the progress of the Force, and gave the Turks timely warning.

At the end of this terrible march they found the main stream of the Euphrates mined, boomed and barricaded ; but even that could not stop them. After what they had gone through, their disposition was not particularly gentle ; and, when they at last closed with the Turks, even the Kurds found that the Infidels could be rough playfellows. The Turks and Kurds ran : the Infidels followed them (" like bloody tigers," the Sheikh of the Muntafik Arabs afterwards said) and captured Nasiriyeh, on the 24th of July. The Turks lost 3,000 men and all their guns and ammunition ; the losses of the British in killed and wounded was just under 1,000. This victory had a tremendous influence on the Arabs ; because Nasiriyeh was the capital of the Muntafik Arabs, the most powerful of all the tribes on the Euphrates. What was left of the defeated Turkish force fell back to Kut on the Tigris.

It will be seen from the map that a strong Turkish force at Kut could still make use of the Shatt el Hai, to strike in the direction of Basra, or could use Kut as a base of operations for an advance across the Persian frontier. Therefore General Nixon, who had

succeeded General Barrett after the battle of Shaiba, thought
that perhaps it would be a good idea to take Kut ; so he ordered
that General Townshend should now advance with his 6th Division
up the Tigris ; this General having already cleared both banks of
the river up as far as Amarah.

Whether at this time it had entered the mind of General
Nixon, or other great minds, that Baghdad should be the ultimate
goal of the " D " Force, is difficult to say. But there is no doubt
—on the authority of published documents—that some great and
ambitious minds, both in England and in India, civil as well as
military, looked upon the capture of Baghdad as desirable, and
not outside the range of possibility.

A certain military politician—of whom there were a great
many—in England, now wrote an article for the public press, in
which he tried to draw a comparison between the present expedition
up the Tigris, for the conquest of Mesopotamia, and the expedition
up the Nile, twenty years before, for the re-conquest of the Sudan.
He very ingeniously pointed out the resemblance between the
advances simultaneously by land and water ; the same strips of
green between the deserts on each side ; the same desire of some-
bodies in authority to call a halt to the advance as the force pushed
on ; and the same constant shifting of the limit, always a little
further on. Then he pointed out how the Sudan was not conquered
until Khartoum fell, and how Mesopotamia could be conquered
only by the fall of Baghdad.

This ingenious and well-meaning amateur strategist
forgot a few items in the programme ; namely, the fact that we
had never set out with the intention of conquering Mesopotamia ;
and that in Egypt we had the Nile Railway and the brains of a
Kitchener ; while, in Mesopotamia, far from having a railway,
we had not sufficient transport for even one Division. But trifles
like these sometimes escape the observation of even the best-
meaning politicians.

At this time also some prominent politicians in the Home
Government began to nibble at the Baghdad bait, so dexterously
thrown by that experienced and wily old sportsman, Von der
Goltz Pasha. They have since told us, both orally and in writing,
that they consulted " experts " on the Baghdad question. One
of these experts published the advice that he gave to the Government. Here are his words, since the words of the wise are precious :
" There is nothing to prevent a well-equipped force of 15,000
to 20,000 men, supported by armoured motor cars and a light
craft flotilla, from occupying Baghdad without serious opposition,
provided of course, that strong Turkish reinforcements are not

sent to the assistance of the original garrison of 50,000 men, now considerably reduced." About the time when this pernicious article appeared in print,* another " powerful article," from the pen of Mr. Horatio Bottomley, appeared under the heading " Roll on, Mighty Russia," just when the Russian soldiers were certainly rolling on, as fast as their legs could carry them, only in the wrong direction.

---

*Land and Water, October 23rd, 1915.

Chapter V.

GENERAL TOWNSHEND'S OPERATIONS.

One of the lessons taught by the history of " D " Force is that there has been no very material change in human nature during the last two thousand years. For the Roman historian, Tacitus, who wrote in the first century of the Christian Era, says : " In War, nothing is more unjust than that all concerned claim its successes for themselves, and throw on others the blame of reverses." He had probably projected his soul into futurity, and foresaw the Mesopotamian Campaigns of Belisarius and Townshend. For even members of the House of Commons, who would have been much puzzled to point out Mesopotamia on a map of the world, claimed as much credit for the initial successes in the Campaign as Uncle Pumblechook, in *Great Expectations*, claimed for the success of the hero of the novel ; but when it came to reverses, their cry was : " Bring out the scapegoat, that we may drive him into the wilderness ! "

Before beginning to deal with General Townshend's operations on the Tigris, we must not overlook certain events which formed the material for what some of our newspapers qualified as a " regrettable incident," and which others passed over in silence.

The tribes inhabiting the country on each side of the Tigris, in its north-and-west bend, between Amarah and Kut are called the Beni Lam Arabs ; those between Amarah and the Persian frontier are the Abu Mohammed Arabs ; and those on the banks of the Shatt el Hai are the Muntafiks. Now there was a tough old warrior of the Beni Lams who had spent the greater part of his life in raiding, robbing and murdering Turks and Persians indiscriminately. At last, the Turkish authorities not only left him alone, but granted him independence, of which he had no need, and a title, Mohammed Pasha, of which he was very proud. Early in 1915, he collected about 6,000 men of the Beni Lams and Abu Mohammeds, whom the Turks supplied with arms and ammunition. He then, in the end of January, led this force across from Amarah, through Hawaizeh, to Ahwaz. To meet this incursion, General Barrett sent Brigadier-General Robinson with a force up the Karun. Robinson, being a gunner, was very scientific in his tactics ; while the only tactics that the old Pasha knew were to go for the enemy and beat him ; which he did. Fortunately for us, he did not cross the Karun ; but, warning his men not to have anything to do with the "devil-tubes" (pipe-line), which he believed to contain explosive machinery, he settled down in the pleasant little valley of the Kherka stream. From here he held watch, like an old tiger in his lair, and kept relays of spies and messengers, towards Mohammerah and Amarah; which were more reliable than the best system of telephones. This is what enabled him, in April, to know all about General Gorringe's 12th Division, which had come to hold the line of the Karun; and to cut up Major Anderson's cavalry detachment, which paid for its carelessness, and ignorance of the country in which it was reconnoitring, with three British officers and 20 sowars.

Now to come back to the Tigris. There is a fairly straight reach of it north of Kurna, for about nine miles; when you get to a place called Bahran. Here it bends sharply to the north-east, makes a loop west and then north-west, to Sakricha. The loop from the east ends at Mazibla, where the river turns to the northwest.

At the end of May, 1915, all the country for miles on each side of the Tigris, between Kurna and Sakricha (nine miles north of Bahran), was under water, with the exception of a sandy ridge between Bahran and Mazibla, and some few dry mounds between Bahran and Kurna. On these mounds the Turks had posted some guns; but the greater part of their force, of about 4,000 men, under Halim Bey, occupied the sandy ridge stretching from Bahran up to Mazibla. On the 10th of May, Townshend was ordered by Nixon " to drive the enemy from his present positions, to capture his guns, to push him up the river, and to occupy Amarah; the operation to be continuous." (The military student should here bear in mind that Amarah was 90 miles from Kurna; and that the thermometer, at this time of the year, never fell below 100° F. day or night, in the theatre of operations).

The force with which Townshend had to carry out his task was composed of the 16th and 17th Infantry Brigades; divisional troops consisting of the Norfolks and 48th Pioneers; a Company of Sappers and Miners; two heavy batteries; a howitzer battery; bridging train and signal company. To convey his men and armament over the floods and river, he had three sloops, four armed launches, and two naval horse-boats, with three of the "Lynch" river steamers to carry troops only. He had also a great number of smaller boats, called "bellums"; some of them protected in front by steel plates; and he had detailed 120 men per battalion to manage these boats. The 17th Brigade, under General Dobbie, carried out the frontal attack on the western bank of the river, under cover of his guns; and the main attack was driven home on the eastern bank, by General Delamain, with the 16th Brigade. Towards the end of the action, Colonel Climo, a very able and experienced officer, took command of the 17th Brigade, replacing Dobbie, invalided.

(The 18th Brigade of this Division had been left to hold the entrenched camp at Shaiba.)

The 103rd Mahrattas, of the 17th Brigade, very bravely attacked and successfully captured one of the principal mounds, with 300 prisoners and two field guns. This regiment and the Oxfords took the Bahran-Mazibla ridge on the 2nd; and the Turks fled back to Amarah, which surrendered to Townshend on the afternoon of the 3rd of June. On the way, he had captured about 300 Turks, with their arms and ammunition, who were slowly moving up the river on lighters and barges.

General Townshend had now good reason to be proud of his success, so far; especially since he had gained it entirely by his own ability and efforts, and had got no assistance whatever from his Commanding Officer, General Nixon. When, on the 18th of May, he sent to Nixon—now officially entitled the "A.C." (Army Commander) in the "D" Force Orders—his memorandum, showing how he intended to beat the Turks in front of him, and take Amarah, the Army Commander, in reply, was good enough to remind him that—

> *The success of the operations depended greatly on the staff work, and on the clearness and completeness of the Operation Orders. These orders were to be framed with great care, and the instructions contained in Field Service Regulations were to be closely followed.*

If such instructions had been written out by the Second-in-Command of a battalion, for the use of a junior Lieutenant preparing for his Promotion Examination, they might be excusable; but for an Army Commander to write them down solemnly, for an officer of Townshend's experience and military qualifications,* was a gross impertinence only to be explained by a mania for meddling interference. Townshend's health was now beginning to break down; and we need not be surprised at this; for you require a very strong mental and physical constitution to overcome constant nagging and worries, especially if you are in a country where you cannot have anything like proper rest or comfort by day or by night, and where you are baked so that your hands and face feel as if they had been skinned and salted.

---

*Townshend had already, some years before this, written and published two very excellent practical works on *Combined Training* and *Operation Orders*, and had kindly presented copies of them to the author.

To recover his health he took a short trip to India ; spent a few days in hospital at Bombay, and went to Simla, where he had an interview with the Commander-in-Chief. He then returned to Mesopotamia, arriving in Basra on the 21st of August. Here he had an interview with Kemball, the chief of Nixon's staff, who said to him : " There must be some sort of natural obstacle covering the left flank of the Turkish position on the Tigris ; but we don't know anything about it."

This obstacle, of which the Staff of the Army Commander knew nothing, is the Suwaikiyah Marsh, twenty-five miles long and twelve miles broad ; called by the Arabs the *Khor al Suwaki*, and stretching from Badran (Badrai) on the north, to within two miles of the Tigris between Umm el Hannah and Sannyat.

At a distance of forty-five miles up the Tigris from Amarah, and on the left bank, is Ali al Gharbi. Here the river bends round by north to west, till it reaches Shaikh Saad, twenty-four miles from Ali al Gharbi, or about 70 miles from Amarah.

While Townshend was in India, General Nixon held a conference in Basra. The most important decision arrived at by this conclave was that two British Brigades should be at once pushed up from their base, Amarah, to Sheikh Saad ; 70 miles away from Amarah, and within 20 miles of the Turkish force under Nureddin, at the position of Es Sinn.

Now every great writer on Strategy, from Jomini and Clausewitz, to Hamley, Foch and Bird, have over and over again warned commanders against a *concentration within striking distance of the enemy.* Yet here we have a decision to concentrate a force within a day's march of the enemy, and four days' march away from its advanced base and reserves.

But Townshend knew better than to attempt to carry this decision into effect. He decided to concentrate his whole force at Ali al Gharbi ; and, with this object in view, he began to send up his forces, from Amarah, on the 1st of September, 1915. He had now, in all, 11,000 fighting men and 30 guns. But he was very short of land transport, so he was tied down to the river.

Chapter VI.

FIRST BATTLE OF ES SINN, OR KUT.

From Shaikh Saad the Tigris runs ten miles north by west ; then bends round north-west, at Umm el Hannah ; and west again, as far as Sanniyat ; the distance between Umm el Hannah and Sanniyat being seven miles. To the north of these two places, roughly parallel to the course of the river, and about two miles from its left bank, runs the edge of the Suwaikiyah Marsh. From Sanniyat the river runs for eight miles south-west, past Nakhailat (on the left bank), to the position of Es Sinn ; where there is now a space of about ten miles between the Tigris and the Suwaikiyah Marsh to the north. But here again, between the river and this large marsh, there are two smaller marshes : the Suwada, about four miles by two, nearer the river ; and the Atabah, about two miles each way, and about three miles north-west of the Suwada Marsh. Running southwards from the river near the Es Sinn position are three old canals, in this order, from east to west : Nasafiyah, Magasis, and Dujailah. The first two join the third about four miles south of Es Sinn, where the Dujailah now runs eastwards, first through sandy mounds and scrub, then through small, shallow marshes. Seven miles south-west of the Es Sinn position, in a southern bend of the river, making a loop about two miles broad by three deep, lies the Arab town of Kut.

On the 15th of September, Townshend had concentrated his force in the broad river-bend a mile east of Sanniyat, opposite the Arab village of Abu Rumman, on the right bank ; about seven miles away from the Turkish trenches at Es Sinn. Here he stayed for ten precious days, waiting for a field battery and a howitzer battery, from Amarah. During these days the Turks went on digging themselves in like moles ; and their commander, Nureddin, got reinforcements which nearly doubled his original force 4,000 strong.

Here, if Townshend, who had every detail of all Napoleon's Campaigns by heart, had only remembered how Marshal Ney lost the battle of Quatre Bras, on the afternoon of the 16th of June, 1815, by waiting for d'Erlon's Division to come up, he would have struck hard and heavy with his 10,000 men, against Nureddin's 4,000, and annihilated them ; even without the help of the two batteries for which he waited. But it is a common fault even of good commanders that they are sometimes cautious in the wrong place.

At this time General Nixon followed the example of Louis the Fourteenth. Whenever the Grand Monarque had reports from his generals that a certain fight was going to be a victory, or that a fortress was sure to surrender within a short time, he came, with his Staff, his Court, and in all his regal glory, to receive the swords of the conquered hostile commanders, or the keys of the surrendered city. In the same way, Nixon now came up, leaving the Army Headquarters at Basra in charge of some luxurious Staff Officers, who had taken British soldiers out of the fighting line, and turned them into batmen and valets : General Sir John Nixon came on the scene of the Battle of Kut.

Townshend had divided his forces into two columns. Column "A" consisted of the 16th (Delamain) and 17th (Hoghton) Brigades, and two batteries ; which started by marching from Abu Rumman along the right, or southern, banks of the Tigris. Column " B " consisted of the 18th (Fry) Brigade, the Divisional Artillery, under General G. B. Smith ; the Divisional Ammunition Column, Supply Column, and the Field Ambulance : to advance partly by water and partly by land, along the left bank.

Three miles south-west of Sanniyat is Nakhailat. Here a bridge was thrown across to the Chahela mounds, on the right bank. Early on the morning of the 26th of September, " B " Column had concentrated a mile and a half south-west of Nakhailat, with its left flank on the river. Column " A," moving along by the right bank, had evidently given the Turkish commander the impression that Townshend's main attack was coming from this quarter. The British General was delighted beyond measure to note the success of his plan, when he saw Nureddin hurrying the troops of his general reserve from their good and safe position, west of the Suwada Marsh, and across their bridge of boats, to the banks of the Dujailah Canal. To confirm Nureddin in his error, Column "A" carried out a sham attack on the right bank, on the morning of the 27th ; while Column " B," with all its guns, opened the real attack along the left bank.

During the afternoon of this day, a number of Sepoys from the 20th Punjabis deserted to the Turks, and informed them that the real attack would not take place on the right, but on the left, bank. This was at once reported to Nureddin, who, however,

44

quietly smiled on hearing it, and remarked to his Staff that the English General was only trying the very old trick of supplying him with false information at the cost of a few sham deserters.

On the evening of the 27th, when darkness came on, Column " A," having left some coolies to light camp fires, wheeled to the right, got quickly into column, and pushed across the bridge to Nakhailat. The 17th Brigade led ; marched eight miles north-west, when they had the Suwaikiyah Marsh on their right, and the Atabah on their left : then moved west and south, getting on the left flank of the Turkish trenches by day-break on the 28th.

When, during this night march, Column "A" had reached a point four miles north-west of Nakhailat, the 16th Brigade broke off, wheeled to the left, and passed through the gap between the Atabah and Suwada Marshes. Having given his men a short rest after their exertions of the night, Delamain dashed at the Turkish trenches in front of him, at half-past seven on the morning of the 28th, with his renowned Dorsets and brave Mahrattas. By midday on the 28th the attack was general all along the line. Nureddin, now finding out his mistake, hurried back his general reserve from the right bank ; but it was too late. The dusk had scarcely set in when the Turks began to run ; and, as the morning of the 29th dawned, there was nothing left in the Es Sinn trenches and positions but dead and wounded Turks. They had lost about 1,800 men, in killed and wounded ; 1,300 prisoners and 17 guns. The British casualties were over 1,400 in killed, wounded, and deserters.

At the Battle of Kurna, Townshend beat the Turks with little difficulty, and followed up their defeated troops into Amarah. And now it occurred to him, and to General Nixon, that he might be in a position to repeat the game ; and, after the Battle of Kut, to follow up the again defeated Turks into Baghdad. The fact is that Townshend had become, like Massena, " the spoiled child of Victory;" and the worst of such spoiled children is that they seem to lose all sense of proportion. Kut was more than Kurna ; Amarah was out of all comparison with Baghdad.

Still, there is no denying that Townshend had every reason to be proud of his victory. To have carried a very strong position, with only a thousand casualties, after weeks of hard marching through a difficult country, under a baking sun, and with in- sufficient transport, was a very fine military performance, rarely equalled in the history of the British Army, and only surpassed by John Nicholson in the days of the Indian Mutiny.*

*And perhaps also by Desaix, who, in 1798, covered 35 miles in one day, in the sands of Egypt, marching and fighting.

So much for the British side ; now let us turn to the other side.

In the first place, it is well to ask : Why did the Turks fight battles at Sahil, Kurna, Shaiba, Nasiriyah, and Kut ? A celebrated, but plain-spoken instructor of Tactics at the Staff College in Deolali —before it removed to Quetta—warned his classes in these words : " You should never look upon your enemy as a bloody idiot." And the Turkish commanders were far from being saguinary imbeciles. In the above-mentioned battles, if we judge by the numbers they employed, their intention could not possibly have been to capture Basra, or to drive back the British into the sea. When we remember the careful preparations they had made for retreat, in each case, before the battle began, we are bound to conclude they must have known that they were going to be beaten. Why then did they stand to fight, and, in some cases, fight very stubbornly ? The plain answer to this is that they were fighting to gain time for their reinforcements to arrive at Baghdad. In the elegant language of the prize ring, they were " sparring for wind." Not only did the American and German Presses state this, after Ctesiphon ; but, before Townshend's failure at Ctesiphon, a neutral paper—the *Revue Militaire Suisse*—plainly warned the British to be careful not to walk into a trap ; and the representative of the American Press in Constantinople foretold that a very unpleasant surprise was being prepared for the British, in addition to the butchery at Gallipoli. At the same time the German newspapers took care to publish, in full, the words of Mr. Asquith, who, speaking of the Mesopotamian Campaign, said in the House of Commons : " I do not think that in the whole course of the War there has been a series of operations more carefully contrived, more brilliantly conducted, and with a better prospect of final success." Why did the German Press repeat this speech ? When a man's enemies begin to pay him compliments, that's the time he should be more careful than ever.

An inspection of the battlefield of Kut on the 29th of September should have taught valuable lessons to wise and prudent commanders who were not too proud to learn. The German officers who had been sent to instruct the Baghdad Army Corps had found apt, keen, and intelligent pupils. Communication trenches, scientifically sited and well built, extended for a length of six miles from the river ; the firing trenches eight to ten feet deep, with periscopes, loopholes, and head-covering. Ranges were marked by flags and discs. Excellent arrangements had been carried out for covering the retirement of the Turks, and for their embarkation on the steamers in rear. There was an elaborate system of observation posts and contact mines ; and the field of fire was everywhere open and level.

The British commanders did not take much notice of these new signs, but went on their way—

> Like boys who, unaware,
> Ranging the woods to start a hare,
> Come to the mouth of the dark lair
> Where, growling low, a fierce old bear
> Lies amidst bones and blood.

Chapter VII.

Some years before the Great War, a Mohammedan gentleman in the Punjab (who had been educated at Winchester and Oxford), a friend of mine, asked my advice with regard to a younger brother of his, who, having finished his University Education, wished to take up a Military career. His ambition soared higher than the rank of Jemadar in a British Indian regiment; so I suggested to him the Turkish Army. As nearly all Turkish officers speak good French, I gave him some books on practical French conversation and military expressions, and a letter of introduction to an influential friend of mine in Constantinople. He got a commission in the Turkish Army; and in the early part of the year 1915 he was on Enver Pasha's Staff.

He wrote to me regularly; and after the battle of Shaiba I got a long letter from him in which he gave me the Turkish point of view on the Mesopotamian Expedition. What this was the following extract will show:—

"You know that the monkeys near the sea coast down in Madras are very fond of oysters. So are the birds, and jackals, and rats, all along that coast. When a fine large oyster comes to enjoy himself on the edge of the tide, his enemies try to snatch him out of his shells. But he catches the birds by their beaks, nips the muzzles of the rats, and grips the jackals' paws, so they are sorry for themselves. Now the monkey comes along; but he places the tip of his tail between what we may call the oyster's jaws. The oyster nips him hard; and the monkey runs away inland, with the oyster hanging on to his tail. The monkey suffers for a time; but, in the end, he cracks the oyster against a stone, and devours him at his ease."

These monkey tactics, contemptible as they may seem, are the oldest and most successful in the history of War. When the mastodon and the woolly elephant roamed the primeval forests, the cave-man fled before them, drawing them on; until they came just under the nicely-balanced rock that he tipped over them. In the same way, old Kutusoff drew on Napoleon, in 1812; and even stood to fight at Borodino, in order that the well-staged tragedy of Moscow might be completely successful. The glorious retreat from the Sambre to the Marne, in 1914, was nothing more than the same old system again, old as the everlasting hills.

As Louis the Fourteenth, after the fall of Namur and the battle of Steinkerk, got and accepted the congratulations and praises which were due to Vauban and Marshal Luxembourg, so was General Sir John Nixon overwhelmed with compliments and felicitated on the results of the battle of Es Sinn, or Kut. Townshend, in the meantime, much encouraged by a wire telling him that " the Cabinet had acquiesced " in his pursuit of the Turks, pushed on with the 18th Brigade and 63rd Field Battery, placing these on board his vessels in the Tigris ; leaving Delamain with the 16th Brigade to occupy Kut ; and Hoghton with the 17th, some three miles behind Delamain, in the Es Sinn position.

It took Townshend six days (28th September to 3rd October) to move, with one brigade and one battery, from Kut to Aziziyah, a distance of sixty miles by river, or forty-five by land. A "pursuit" at the rate of nine miles a day would be called something quite different by a Pappenheim, a Murat, or a Ney. But Townshend's soldiers *had to wait for their own special cooking-pots !* When, in 1857, John Nicholson marched down from the Indus to Delhi, in the worst time of the year, at the rate of 25 miles a day, none of *his* Sikhs who had any regard for their lives would have suggested to him that they should halt for cooking-pots. But there were no Nicholsons, nor Clives, nor Robertses, in Mesopotamia.

During his pursuit, Townshend received a long official letter, enclosing an unofficial communication, by post, from General Nixon. The former contained the writer's " appreciation of the situation." It stated that there were two courses open to the British Force ; namely, to discontinue the pursuit, or to go on with it, into Baghdad. The other letter warned Townshend that a defeat or retreat would be fatal to British prestige in the East, and might also interfere with Townshend's chances of promotion. This was like the University don who chanced to hear an undergraduate blaspheming, and said to him : " Not only do you peril your immortal soul, sir, but you'll have to pay a fine of ten shillings to the University authorities ! "

All this time there was ringing in Townshend's ears the last sentence that Sir Beauchamp Duff ever spoke to him : " Not one inch beyond Kut shall you go unless you have a force of forty thousand men ! " He was getting orders, instructions, directions, and suggestions, from General Nixon's Staff, all day and all night ; until at last—at which nobody can be surprised—he shot off a wire to the Headquarters at Basra : " Is General Nixon commanding this operation in person, or does he intend me to command it ? " Every soldier, from the Field Marshal down to the Lieutenant who commands a platoon on a field day, will sympathise here with General Townshend.

By the end of October he had concentrated his whole force, 14,000 strong, at Aziziyah. Some of his Indian regiments had been recruited up to full strength ; and he said of this new accession of force : " I have never seen such a wretched class of recruits in the whole of my Indian experience."

One whole battalion he had to get rid of and send down to Basra, on account of their insubordination, treachery, cowardice and desertions. Anybody acquainted with the Indian Army knows that the Sepoy battalion is what its British Officers have made it ; and it is always possible to tell what its character must be, in peace or war, when one knows the personality and mentality of its British Officers. When a British Officer is so lost to a sense of duty, self-respect, or patriotism, that he looks upon an appointment to an Indian battalion merely as a stepping-stone to some snug and luxurious Staff billet, he has made a mistake in his choice of a profession.

A Turkish force, 10,000 strong, under the command of Nureddin Pasha, stood strongly entrenched, on the left bank of the Tigris, at Ctesiphon, thirty-two miles north-west of Aziziyah ; with Zeur, eight miles south-east of Ctesiphon, as an advanced post, held by 2,000 men and six guns ; this covered again by a mixed camel-and-cavalry corps, about 1,800 strong, at Kutunie, three miles south-west of Zeur.

On the night of 27/28th October, Townshend marched, with a force of about 12,000 men, against these advanced positions, and cleared them of the Turks, who fell back leisurely on their main position at Ctesiphon.

The Battle of Ctesiphon, November 22nd, 23rd, 1915.

General Townshend spent the first two weeks of November in making preparations for a decisive attack on the Turkish position at Ctesiphon. It would be an injustice to this able commander to suggest that he wasted valuable time. But the military student cannot help noting that all through this campaign the commanders do not seem to have fully appreciated the value of not only days, but of hours, and of minutes, in military operations. How different from Townshend's great model, Napoleon ! At the critical moment in the battle of Austerlitz, he calls up Marshal Soult, and asks him : " Comment vous faut-il de temps, Maréchal, pour couronner les hauteurs de Pratzen ? " " Moins de vingt minutes," answers Soult. "Attendons un quart d'heure," said Napoleon.*

*" How long would you take to cover the heights of Pratzen, Marshal ? "
" Less than twenty minutes."
" Let us wait for fifteen minutes."

The Turkish position at Ctesiphon was somewhat similar to that at Es Sinn ; but it was stronger, and had two lines of entrenchments. The river Tigris, on the west and south of the position, has the shape of one of those large hooks for sea-fishing, with a bend forward (eastwards) at the top ; the barbed point facing north-east, at Bustan ; Ctesiphon on the east, half way up the shank of the hook, and Kusaibah at the top. The first line of entrenchments ran from the bottom of the loop of the hook for nearly six miles to the north-east ; then, a little more than two miles behind this line, nearly parallel to it, ran the second line, to a mound, or mamelon, called Yesi, two miles east of Kusaibah ; and, from here, three miles further on to the north-east, to the rough road, thorugh the scrub, which leads by the bank of an old canal, from Kut, across the Diyalah river, to Baghdad. There was a bridge of boats just about half way between Kusaibah and Ctesiphon. The first line of trenches and redoubts was held by 2,000* Turks, some of them dismounted cavalry. A strong redoubt at the north-eastern end of the line, two miles south of Yesi, was occupied by 300 infantry. The second line was held by 2,000 infantry ; a reserve of about 5,000 was posted about Kusaibah ; and a detached force of about 3,000 was pushed forward in the direction of Lajj. The few entrenchments on the right bank, west of the loop, was held by a mixed force of Arabs and Turks, infantry and cavalry, about 2,000 strong. The reinforcements which Townshend had received by the end of the second week in November brought up his force to a strength of about 16,000 ; while the enemy in trenches in front of him was about 12,000.

Townshend's tactics in this battle were similar to those employed by him at Es Sinn. He divided his forces into four columns : Column " A," under General Delamain to strike at the enemy's centre ; Column " B," under General Hamilton, on Delamain's right, to support the latter and drive home his attack ; Column" C," under General Hoghton, with the Divisional Artillery and Troops, on Delamain's left, that is, between him and the river ; then, the " Flying Column," including the Cavalry Brigade and " S " Battery, R.H.A., under General Melliss, which was to swing round wide on Hamilton's right, and " cut off the retreat of the flying Turks from their bridges over the Diyalah."

About eighty years before this time, a British General, named MacCaskill, made exactly similar arrangements, to cut off the retreat of his Afghan opponents, commanded by Dost Mohammed ; at a place called Purwandarrah. And so strong did he make his enveloping force, at the expense of his centre, that the Afghan

---

*In the figures given here, the Arab irregulars are not included.

leader at once detected the mistake; and, sweeping forward with his cavalry, cut MacCaskill's force clean in two. It is always waste of time to make arrangements for selling the skin of the bear before you have killed the animal.

Townshend tried no tricks this time, to lead his opponent astray, by any feint attacks along the right bank of the Tigris. And the reason is that he wanted to get to Baghdad as quickly as possible. But Nureddin also knew well what was the wish and intention of the British General. He knew that Townshend would pursue the same battle tactics with which he had succeeded at Es Sinn; and he made up his mind that, as far as *he* was able to prevent it, those tactics would not be successful a second time.

At half past one on the afternoon of the 21st of November, Townshend issued his orders for the attack. In them he explained his plan : to contain the front of the enemy with a minimum force, while executing a turning movement against his left flank and rear, with a maximum force. General Hoghton, with 3,500 men, was to carry out the frontal attack. On a frontage of about a mile, he pushed forward from Lajj (seven miles south-east of Bustan), between two and three o'clock on the afternoon of the 21st. At daylight next morning he was to attack the trenches in the loop, sweep through them, and assist the armed ships which were following the force up the river.

At half-past seven on the morning of the 22nd, General Hamilton, with 3,000 men, was to start on a turning movement of about ten miles; first north-east, then west, with Kusaibah for its objective. The Flying Column, 2,000 strong, under General Melliss, was to work in co-operation with Hamilton, two miles on the outer flank of the latter.

The main force, or General Reserve, under Delamain, 4,500 strong, was to be, by daylight, on the 22nd, in position about two miles east of the redoubt which closed the first line of trenches on the north-east.

The weakest point of the enemy's position was that if Townshend's attack against his left should prove successful, the Turks in the trenches would have no way of retreat. It was to meet such a contingency that Nureddin posted his strong reserve conveniently at Kusaibah.

It is well to note here that the tactical arrangements made by Townshend, on this occasion, are open to the same objections as the Grand Tactics of the German Chief Staff in their great sweep through Belgium in August, 1914. The enveloping force, with its Cavalry, was, in both cases, confided to two independent commanders.

Townshend seems to have had a regular mania for night marches. He should have remembered that, in the South African War, Buller, Gatacre, Methuen, and Roberts, employed night marches and night attacks, not one of which was successful. Nearly all of his troops spent the night of the 21st/22nd on the march and digging. Now no troops will ever do themselves full justice unless they have had a fair share of natural refreshing sleep. And this is particularly true of Oriental soldiers, who, unless they have their sleep, are always limp and spiritless next day. British troops, and soldiers of Anglo-Saxon blood, on the contrary, have often proved that they can march all night ; and the very want of sleep seems to make them fight fiercer when the daylight comes. At the Battle of the Wilderness, on the morning of the 5th May, 1864, the Texan Brigade of General Lee's Army, having covered eighteen miles of very difficult country during the night, came into action, at the double, against General Hancock's left flank, and rolled up a whole Federal Division. " We collapsed like a wet blanket," said General Hancock.

If Townshend's men had been all British, his night-marching would have had better results ; but British they were not. And the night of the 21st/22nd was bitterly cold, with icy blasts from the Pusht-i-Kuh range on the east.

About six o'clock on the morning of the 22nd, Hoghton's column—on the left, nearest the river—pushed forward, very cautiously and slow ; and when the sun had dispersed the morning mist, shortly before eight o'clock, the two leading battalions of the Column (The Oxford and Bucks Light Infantry, and the 119 N.I.) found themselves within a mile of the low brown mounds which marked the position of the Turkish trenches. It cannot be said that the guns behind him assisted Hoghton very much in his advance ; so he halted his column, and sent out scouts to reconnoitre his front.

In the meantime Column " B " had got into position five miles to the north, about a mile and a half east of Yesi; and its commander, Hamilton, not hearing anything of Hoghton's attack, which was to be his signal to move forward, became impatient, and asked Townshend for permission to go ahead. This was granted ; Column " B " and the Flying Column on its right dashed forward at about half-past eight. Had this been done before Hamilton had delayed to wait for permission, the surprise of the Turks would have been completely successful in this part of the field. But unfortunately in this Campaign we too frequently find cases of hesitation, almost amounting to fear, on the part of subordinates, to accept responsibility.

The last time that the great Von Moltke addressed the students of the Kriegsakademie, his closing words were : " The determining factor in War is the initiative of the subordinate leaders." It is a matter for regret that this factor played but a very small part in the Mesopotamian Campaign.

The Indian Cavalry Regiments, 7th, 16th, and 33rd, scattered the enemy's cavalry which had been posted on the left of the second line of Turkish trenches, north of Yesi ; but the 33rd had to turn back, to protect the transport of the Flying Column, on which a horde of predatory Arab horsemen had just swooped down. The men of the other two cavalry regiments now dismounted, and pushed forward, with Hamilton's infantry on their left ; the advance being here well supported by the 76th Field Battery and " S " Battery of the Royal Horse Artillery. They gained ground slowly until about midday, when they were held up by the hail from the Turkish trenches and guns.

At about nine o'clock in the morning, Delamain launched out from Column "A" a force 2,000 strong, under the able command of the gallant and experienced Climo. This force, pushing forward on a frontage of 600 yards—Gurkhas in the first line—like a whirl-wind, swept the Turks before them, covering a distance of three miles in an hour and a half, and fighting every yard of the way. Their objective was a redoubt in the strongest part of the first line of Turkish trenches ; which Townshend, for some reason, called the V.P. or " Vital Point." But it proved afterwards that this was by no means the vital point of the position ; which— if we are to have a " vital point "—was rather the Yesi mamelon, or the mound behind the high old arch at Ctesiphon.

It was about eleven o'clock when Delamain brought up his Dorsets and Mahrattas to hammer home the success so well gained by Climo. And now was the time that Nureddin showed his generalship. He did not trouble himself about Hoghton's advance, or the heavy attack on his left flank. He could see that Delamain's was the Main Attack ; so, collecting all his reserves, he dashed down, from the north-west, and began to envelop Delamain's force on both flanks.

Just then Townshend rode on to the scene, and saw at once through Nureddin's game. To counter it, he ordered Hoghton to wheel his force to the right, so as to clear Delamain's left flank. Hoghton obeyed ; but in doing so he had to execute the most dangerous movement in War ; that is, a flank march across the enemy's front. It was lucky for him that the Turks on the left flank of his movement took no advantage of this rare opportunity ; but merely contented themselves with pumping in their bullets, on an unresisting, slowly-moving mass, at a distance of about

800 yards. When he got into touch with Delamain's left, his men made a right shoulder forward, and faced the Turks again.

Now the battle joined all along the whole front, continuing, with varying fortune, till about four o'clock in the afternoon. Then some of the Indian regiments began to totter and break. All the efforts of Townshend himself, of Delamain, and of the gallant and energetic Kemball, could not keep them in their ranks, nor rally them. At five o'clock, Townshend ordered the fighting to cease.

By this time Nureddin had also had enough of it. He withdrew what was left of his force to his second line of trenches ; where they lay all through the bitterly cold night which followed the day of battle.

In this fight, the British lost over 5,000 in killed, wounded and missing ; the Turkish losses, all told, were about 7,500.

Chapter VIII.

THE RETREAT FROM CTESIPHON.

Any man who is lacking in decision, who cannot make up his mind in time of a sudden and unexpected crisis—" at a pinch," as it is commonly said—must never expect to be a successful commander in operations where " it is the unexpected that always happens." General Walter Kitchener—who had the misfortune of being overshadowed by his more eminent brother, "Al Sardar al Kebir," (the Great Sardar)—was a soldier sound and practical as ever served in the British Army. He always tried to instil into his subordinates the tremendous advantages of a man being able to arrive at a decision quickly. I have heard him say (in a Lecture) : " A wrong decision, quickly arrived at and carried out with energy, is more likely to be successful than a correct decision arrived at too late."*

When General Townshend got the surprise of his life at Ctesiphon, he could not make up his mind ; for three days and nights he could not arrive at a decision as to what was best to be done. It was this fatal wavering and indecision which led to the siege, starvation, and surrender of Kut.

Like General Lee, on the morning after the drawn battle of Antietam, and General Gough on the morning after his defeat at Chilianwala, Townshend for some time thought of renewing the battle ; and General Nixon—" watching the proceedings on behalf of the Crown," as they say in the Law Courts—took it upon himself to send out a reconnaissance in force ; on the same principle that impelled Diogenes to go rolling his tub up and down the streets of the City while the other citizens were defending the walls.

But, having been informed by Delamain, Hoghton and Hamilton, of the heavy casualties in his force, Townshend, for the present, contented himself in concentrating by the river and evacuating his wounded. The Turks, meantime, kept dribbling

---

*At the great manœuvres of the Northern Army (India) in 1903, he, with Sir Bindon Blood, was Umpire in Chief. He was as deaf as a post, but he was rather sensitive about it ; he pretended that he could hear quite well. On the second day of the manœuvres, an umpire (Major George, Madras Cavalry) came galloping up to him, and, in a towering rage, said : " Colonel B—— has just called me a —— —— because I put his regiment out of action ! " His A.D.C. became apoplectic, and General Blood was seized with a violent fit of coughing. But General Kitchener beamed and said : " Oh, capital, capital ! I like a man who makes up his mind quickly."

back into their second line of trenches. General Khalil Pasha arrived at Khusaibah; having been sent down hurriedly from Baghdad, by Von der Goltz, to urge Nureddin to assume the offensive. But a change from the defensive to the offensive takes some time to carry out; and Townshend, who knew this well, should have taken advantage of the reprieve. Still he did not withdraw the last of his troops from their useless positions, in the first Turkish line of trenches in the river loop, until about two o'clock on the night of the 24th/25th.

There has been a good deal said and written about the abnormal difficulties which Townshend had to overcome on account of the extraordinary vividness of the *mirage* in the Tigris plains. But surely the mirage must have been just as puzzling to a Turkish as to a British Commander. Anybody who has travelled for some time in Mesopotamia, and who makes good use of his eyes, ought to be able to recognise a mirage after he has seen a few of them. In the mirage there is never any life or movement; the branches of the palms do not wave in the wind; the water does not ripple or roll; and it is impossible to detect exactly the points where the edge of the lake or pool meets the land.

On the afternoon of the 24th—two days after the battle— Townshend told Kemball that " he did not propose to retire until it became necessary to do so "; while, at the same time, Khalil, only a few miles away, was repeating to Nureddin the Turkish equivalent of Lady Macbeth's " Oh, infirm of purpose, give *me* the daggers ! "

In order that the movements of Townshend's retreat may be clearly followed it must be borne in mind what the distances between his halting-places are; these distances being given as the crow flies, not following the bends of the river, and over terrain, be it remembered, which was not broken or intersected by any streams, old canal beds, or marshes. From Bustan (by Ctesiphon) to Lajj, eight miles; Lajj to Aziziyah, twenty miles; and Aziziyah to Kut, fortyfive miles; the whole distance being, by his route, well under eighty miles.

He took three days to get clear from Bustan to Lajj. Having got so far, he wrote to Nixon : " Here I remain, and demonstrate up the right bank almost immediately."[*] After this letter, he wired to Nixon, that the second line of entrenchments at Ctesiphon were then being reoccupied by the Turkish force. Therefore, on this date, the 26th, the enemy was eighteen miles behind; and, as

---

[*]My Campaign in Mesopotamia, p. 188.

57

far as we know, had then no intention of following him up. He started making entrenchments here at Lajj ; and, for some reason, which is not apparent, threw a bridge over the river here, and sent half a battalion to the right bank, to throw up and hold a bridge-head. He had probably intended to cross his whole force to the right bank, so as to have the river between himself and the enemy ; but, anyhow, he made no use of the bridge. Late on that afternoon, it occurred to him that "Aziziyah was a more desirable place in every way "† ; and he marched away from Lajj on the night of the 27th, reaching Aziziyah on the 29th ; having taken six days to cover the thirty miles from the battlefield. From here he sent another wire to Nixon, in which we find this burst of optimism : " Kut is a strategic point we are bound to hold . . . . . Should the enemy follow me to Kut, so much the better. We ought to destroy him in that case." He remained in Aziziyah during the whole of the 29th, waiting for a steamer which was to come and carry away the stores of clothing and equipment. But the steamer did not turn up ; so he made a heap of the stores and set fire to it. To add to his worries, he now got an urgent message from Nixon, who was at Kut, and who wanted to get safely away down the river as soon as possible. Would Townshend send some troops to re-open the lines of communication, which had been cut ? In reply, Townshend sent General Melliss and the 30th Brigade to clear a safe exit for the Army Commander and his Staff.

At nine o'clock on the morning of the 30th, Townshend's force started out from Aziziyah, and got as far as Umm al Tamal (nine miles) by noon. Here the advanced guard of the pursuing Turks was first observed, at a distance of about four miles behind the force. Townshend would, and should, have kept on the move, if he had not had to stay and guard the ships in the river, on his right. He should have sunk the ships, which would have prevented the Turks from making use of the river to follow him up ; strength-ened his force with the personnel of the ships, and pushed forward with all his might.

At Umm al Tamal he fought a rearguard action, and even carried out a spasmodic offensive against his pursuers, employing his favourite tactics of a holding attack, in front, combined with an enveloping attack on the flank ; with which the Turks must have been quite familiar by this time. This action cost him 500 men killed and wounded. He tells us* of the high fighting qualities shown by his troops in this affair, " unshaken by the fierce fighting they had undergone at Ctesiphon " ; and when the fight was over

---

*My Campaign in Mesopotamia, p. 195.
†My Campaign in Mesopotamia, p. 189.

he contined his march, by echelons of brigades, until he reached Shadie (Shidhai) thirty-six miles from his starting-point of the morning. He calls this a " record march," and it is certainly a very fine performance. But why had he already taken *five days to cover only* 28 *miles* ?

He left Shadie on the morning of the 2nd December, and arrived in Kut early on the 3rd.

Chapter IX.

IN KUT.

During his retreat down the river after the battle of Ctesiphon General Townshend was followed, but not pursued, by mounted bodies of Turks and Arabs. Turkish infantry, in rear of these, came up with him, as already mentioned, near Umm al Tumal, where he turned at bay and hit them hard. But the mounted troops did not directly attack the retreating force; they moved rather widely parallel to it, especially on the east of the Tigris; and by means of mounted scouts they kept themselves well informed as to every move of the retreating British force.

The words used in the German wireless, sent out for the benefit of German propagandists in Persia, were: "Our forces herded in the retreating English, so that they were forced to take up the Kut position." (The verb which I have translated "herded" is, in the original, *lenken*, which means to steer a boat, to direct a horse by the reins, and so forth.)

Baghdad had not been taken; and the question here is, who drove General Townshend forward towards Baghdad, with a body of troops altogether insufficient for the task he had to perform? He was ordered to go and take Baghdad with one Division; a forlorn hope, if ever there was one. He went, and ran headlong into four Turkish Divisions*; lost heavily; retreated, somewhat slowly, though in good order, to Kut; and remained boxed up there until he was starved into surrender.

That section of the London Press which was interested in supporting the political Party then in power did its very utmost to throw the whole blame of the Mesopotamian failure on the Indian Government. One of its leading organs said :—
"Who is responsible for the insane idea of attempting to take Baghdad with 20,000 men?" (General Townshend had nothing like 20,000 men). "We are bound to say that this Baghdad gamble very strongly resembles the Gallipoli gamble; and its authorship ought to be probed to the core. If the Government of India are the true and only begetters of the affair, there is something rotten in the Government of India; and, in view of their vast

---

*A Turkish Division is not at all as large as a Division in the British Army, being rarely more than 6,000 strong, sometimes only 4,000.

responsibilities, the country has a right to demand a ruthless scrapping of the incompetence at the top which must be held guilty. The people who planned this side-show are manifestly convicted bunglers. We fear there is a tendency in this War to give incompetence too long a rope. Something is wrong at the top."

We have surely come across this sort of language before : Antient Pistol of the " Gallic Wars." As a comparison has been established with the Gallipoli " gamble "—as the writer calls that hideous and useless butchery of brave men—there can be no harm in calling attention to the place where the responsibility for Gallipoli ultimately lies.

On the 2nd of November, 1915, the man " at the top," said, in the House of Commons :—

" If anybody is responsible for the initiation of this enterprise in the Dardanelles, nobody is more responsible than I."

Did our Antient Pistol now demand " a ruthless scrapping of the incompetence at the top ? " Not a bit of it. He burst into ecstasies—

" Give me thy fist,
Thy spirits are most tall."

as though he " at the top " had said something to be proud of.

But, on that very date, the 2nd of November, the man at the top said something more, which helps us to explain the Baghdad problem. Before making his apologies for the Dardanelles failure, he very skilfully switched on his remarks to Mesopotamia. He joyfully asserted that General Nixon was " within measurable distance of Baghdad," and added : " I do not think that in the whole course of the War, there has been a series of operations more carefully contrived, more brilliantly conducted, and with a better prospect of ultimate success." Then, before the taste of the sugar was off the pill, he undertook the difficult and disagreeable task of explaining the fiasco of the Dardanelles. And it is here we get the solution of the Mesopotamian problem.

Towards the end of October, the Home Government were beginning to tremble on account of Gallipoli. It had begun to dawn on them that we were going to be beaten there ; and a retreat from Gallipoli would be altogether different from the honourable and immortal retreat from Mons to the Marne. The public, who were not gagged or afraid, would begin to ask unpleasant questions about it ; and it was concluded that a good set-off would be a crop of laurels raised in the soil of the Tigris sands and marshes.

Up to the present the Turks had always been beaten at every battle in Mesopotamia ; and Townshend's victory at Kut came as a regular godsend, shedding on our Home Government a bright ray of hope. In such a case, of course no Government official would issue clear, or emphatic, or direct orders. They could not say to the Indian Government, in plain English, " We have made a terrible and costly mistake in this Dardanelles business. Don't you think you could help us to draw public attention away from it by the successful capture of Baghdad, and you may depend upon us to do the trumpet-blowing for you at Home ? " Now, given a British Commander sitting at Basra, who very evidently miscalculated the military situation, and whose Staff confessed their blank ignorance of a military obstacle, a swamp, covering near four hundred square miles in the immediate theatre of operations ; given a Government at Home, ignorant of the most elementary principles of War, hopelessly ignorant of physical and climatic conditions in the theatre of operations, and very eager to cover up the failure of the Dardanelles with the laurels of Baghdad ; we have the solution of the tragedy of Kut, and the transport of British Forces to Mesopotamia, who would have shortened the War by many months if they had been employed in France.

Let there be no manner of doubt about this ; the reasons for the advance from Kut to Baghdad were entirely *political* ; the move was altogether unjustifiable from a military point of view. As a military enterprise, it was one of the maddest and worst ever undertaken in warfare ; almost criminal in its stupidity.

Neither General Townshend nor the Indian Government deserves the blame or the shame of it ; the disaster of Kut, like the slaughter in the Khoord Kabul Pass (1842), the terrible loss of British lives in the Crimean War, the defeat of Maiwand, the disastrous surprise at Wano, and the massacre in the Tochi Valley, have been all *directly due to the meddling interference of politicians in matters military* ; and in no case has the officer or the soldier been to blame. Our greatest conquerors in the East, Clive, Coote, Wellesley, Gough, Nicholson, and Lawrence, would have never been successful if they had had politicians to interfere with their plans. But it must be acknowledged that the politicians, in some cases, got their own back ; when, for instance, they worried Clive into cutting his throat, and hounded down Warren Hastings into misery and beggary.

The politicians have the great advantage of being in the position to decide, at the end of a Campaign, what soldiers should be rewarded with titles, honours, and money ; but, as the Duke of Wellington said, " there's no damned nonsense about *merit* in it." In these times, neither a Marlborough nor a Napoleon would have the smallest chance of distinction, in comparison with the nominal soldier whose first care is to keep a good " press agent," to get himself written up by some presumptuous and mischievous blockhead, who knows less of Strategy than of the depths of the Pacific Ocean, and whose experience in Logistics has been limited to a Margate excursion train.

Honours and titles are the rewards of successful soldiers, no matter how the success has been gained ; but there is still one thing to be thankful for : the soldier who wants a title does not deserve it, and the soldier who deserves it does not want it.

On the morning of the 7th October, when Delamain's officers had turned out of their billets at Kut, to fall in for the march to Ctesiphon, they breathed deep sighs of relief on getting into the open air once more. Many of them had been so unwise as to billet in the *Khans*, or coffeehouses, where they left the mosquitos in a state of bloated gluttony, and which were alive with insects, cockroaches, and rats.

Now when the average sober man, on waking up in the morning, and opening the only eye which is not bunged up by the bite of a sandfly, sees one of his socks moving across the ceiling and his khaki shirt slowly crawling up the wall, while his trousers are performing a lively jazz on the clay floor, covered with cockroaches, he will jump out of bed, and stamp about—which will remind him of walking on sea-weed—and swear that he will never come to *that* place again. But when the fates and the fortune of War have so willed it that he is compelled to violate his vow, we must not be at all surprised if he is not quite so happy and contented as if he was lodged in the Ritz or the Savoy. When this was the case with the officers, we can perhaps form some idea as to the feelings and sentiments (and language) of the private soldiers in Townshend's Force when the General had decided to take refuge in Kut.

He should never have gone there. As an experienced soldier and profoundly learned in Military History, he should have done anything sooner than follow the pernicious examples of Mack at Ulm (1805), Bazaine at Metz (1870), Osman Pasha at Plevna (1877), and Stoessel at Port Arthur (1905). But, just as one lucky bet on the race-course will afflict the man who has won it with an incurable mania for backing horses, until he is ruined ; in the same way, Townshend's successful holding out in Chitral, during the siege of this place, gave him the false belief that he could also hold out in Kut ; and made him overlook the facts that the Turks were as different from the Yussufzais as the Western Himalaya from the low plains of the Tigris.

But, it may be asked, what else could he have done ? Well, from Bustan, near Ctesiphon, to Kut, is eighty miles in a straight line ; all flat, and without any obstacle whatever on the way. When his Brigadiers handed in the reports of their casualties, at nine o'clock on the morning of the 23rd November, he must have known that he could not now fight the Turks with any prospect of success ; especially as he knew that Nureddin had received reinforcements during the previous afternoon. He should have then sent his ships down the river ; let them sink or swim. The first care of a Commander should always be the safety of the Force committed to his charge. His men could march, and fight, thirty-six miles in one day, as they proved at Umm el Tumal. So that, by going twenty miles a day, he could have easily gained Shaikh Saad on the 30th of November. No man knew better than he the strength of the Es Sinn position, which he would have neutralised by pushing on to Shaikh Saad ; and, as it turned out, the Turks following him would not have reached this place before the 8th of December, at the earliest. By this time, he would have had more than a week at Sheikh Saad ; and Nureddin, finding him there, would very probably get behind the Es Sinn lines again, and stay in them until he was driven out.

Townshend informs us* that his Force covered a distance of *seventy-six* miles on the 1st and 2nd of December. If he did this, he must have made many twistings and turnings on the way ; for the whole distance, in a straight line, between Aziziyah and Kut, is well under fifty miles.

It was not until the 8th of December that the Turks began to invest Kut. This was a clear fourteen days after Townshend's withdrawal from the battlefield of Ctesiphon. If, during this precious time, he had moved his force at the rate of only *twelve* miles a day, he would have been safe, at Ali al Gharbi, on the 7th of December, with the main Turkish Force sixty miles away, behind him.

The question of the strategical value of Kut is ably summed up by General Bird,† in the following words :—

" The whole strategical problem resolves itself into the question as to whether the effect likely to be produced by the action of a British detachment being at Kut, would compensate for the risk that would be incurred by the British of defeat in detail ; or, what amounts to the same thing, whether the cause of the British would be better served by keeping, or endeavouring to keep, their forces

---

*My Campaign in Mesopotamia, p. 200.
†A Chapter of Misfortunes, p. 99.

united, or by deliberately splitting them into two portions. Tactically, Kut was, on the whole, not suitable for the purpose with which it was occupied. Strategically the balance of argument is also against this policy. But it has on occasion been pursued with success—as at Prague in 1757,and at Ladysmith in 1899-1900."

On questions like this, the decision of the successor of Hamley and Henderson is final ; and there is no doubt that this will be also the decision of the British military historian of the future.

Chapter X.

ATTEMPTS TO RELIEVE KUT.

Townshend had with him in Kut 13,000 men, and about 4,000 Indian followers. He was not badly off in the way of ammunition ; he had rations for his troops for sixty days ; also grain for thirty days, and fodder for seventeen days.

The Turkish besieging force was 15,000 strong, with thirty-six guns.*

When Townshend's reports had reached Army Headquarters, Mesopotamia, General Nixon decided to organize a relieving force, which was to be placed under the command of a very gallant and experienced soldier, Lieutenant-General Aylmer. This force, officially called the Tigris Corps, was to be concentrated at Ali al Gharbi, early in January, 1916. General Aylmer estimated that he would have to deal with a hostile force of about 40,000 men and 100 guns ; but the Turkish strength against him never reached anything like this figure.†

The Tigris Corps was to consist of the 7th and 3rd Divisions, and other troops. It was decided that this Force, consisting of 15,000 infantry and cavalry, and forty guns, should be concentrated at Ali al Gharbi by the 3rd of January. If, simultaneously with Aylmer's relieving attack, Townshend could manage to carry out a sortie with 7,000 men, there was reason to hope that the relief would be effected. But it was necessary that this should be done without any waste of time ; for by the middle of January the rains were to be expected ; the Tigris would begin to rise ; the whole country would be under water, and the swampy ground absolutely impassable.

Instead, however, of concentrating all his efforts and employing every available man and gun for the relief of Kut, General Nixon, towards the end of December, sent off a force, under General

---

*From February, 1915, to June, 1916, part of my duties was to translate, for the benefit of Army Headquarters, India, the French, German and Russian messages picked up by the wireless station in Karachi. The German messages relating to events in Mesopotamia proved to be fairly accurate.

†The German accounts of the Turkish strength here, sent out by wireless, and picked up by me in Karachi, agree with the figures given in his book, *Von Balkan nach Bagdad*, by Von Gleich, Chief of the Staff to General Von der Goltz. The total strength was never more than 25,000.

Gorringe, against a few thousand Arab vagabonds who were supposed to be concentrating up the Euphrates for an attack on Nasiriyeh.

Townshend had beaten back a heavy Turkish attack on the 24th December; and Aylmer now enquired of him as to how he could assist by a sortie, on or about the 10th of January. His reply was not encouraging; he was very anxious to know from Aylmer the strength of the relieving force. Aylmer informed him that it was to be two Divisions and a Cavalry Brigade.

The advanced guard of the Tigris Force at Ali al Gharbi was under the command of General Younghusband. On the 2nd of January, Aylmer arrived here; ordered Younghusband to push forward to Sheikh Saad, and made preparations to advance from Ali al Gharbi with the rest of the Force on the 6th of January.

By this time General Nixon had discovered that the Force which he had sent under Gorringe to Nasiriyeh could not find any enemy in front of them; so, acting on the advice of General Aylmer, he now sent Gorringe's Force up the Shatt al Hai, " to create a diversion," and to spread reports that they were the advance guard of a strong force moving up to attack the Turks, from the south. Many were the efforts made during this Campaign to mystify and mislead the Turks; but they rarely succeeded, because the sources of information for the Turks were far more punctual, correct, and better organised than those of the British.

On the evening of the 6th of January, Younghusband at Sheikh Saad was warned, by telegram from Aylmer, to be very careful not to commit himself to a fight with the Turks. But the Turks gave Younghusband no choice in the matter. They fiercely attacked him on the morning of the 7th, and kept up the fight all that day and night, and all next day. Their trenches were on both sides of the river. Of Younghusband's Force, the 28th Brigade attacked on the right bank, with the Cavalry on their left flank; the 35th Brigade attacked on the left bank, nearest the river, with the 19th and 21st Brigades on their right.

During the night of the 8th/9th, and early on the morning of the 9th of January, the Turks fell back, and took up a new position on the right bank of a broad stream which falls into the Tigris, six miles north-west of Sheik Saad. (This is called the *Wady*, which means "River Valley.") There was no attempt to pursue the Turks; for it cannot be correctly said that they were beaten in this battle. Never had they fought so well in this Campaign, up to the present; not even at Ctesiphon. The casualties in Younghusband's Force was over 4,000; more than twenty per cent. of the Force.

About this time there was a rumour of the advance of a Russian Force, coming through Persia to join hands with the British ; but it was only a rumour, and came to nothing.

About two miles west of the Turkish position on the Wady is the issue from the Hannah defile, which was now getting narrower each day by the rains which filled the Suwaikiyah Marsh. (It will be remembered that the Es Sinn position is seven miles south-west of the western issue of the Hannah defile.)

The Turkish Force behind the Wady was about 11,000 strong ; the strength of Aylmer's Force was about the same figure. But the Turks were behind entrenchments. Aylmer attacked them on the 13th of January ; employing tactics similar to those of Townshend at Es Sinn and Ctesiphon : Younghusband to carry out the enveloping attack against their left flank. During the night of the 13th/14th the Turks cleared out of the Wady position, and fell back to the mouth of the defile.

On the 14th, Aylmer's bad luck began, when the rain came down in torrents, accompanied by a bitterly cold driving wind. It did not cease for a moment all that day or the following night ; and the ground became so sodden that no movement of troops was possible. On the night of the 15th, Aylmer sent by telegram a very sound suggestion to Townshend ; and, of course, sent a copy of it to General Nixon at Headquarters. He said :—

" On the right bank below Kut there are not more than 2,000 of the enemy, and the rains have made the crossing of the Hai difficult for transport. The best thing that Townshend could do is to cross the river during the night with all available men, and march round Es Sinn on the right bank. I would cross here with one Division and a Cavalry Brigade and bring him back. The opportunity is now favourable, and may cease directly the enemy sends troops down the right bank, which may be very soon."

But General Nixon would not hear of this ; he ordered Aylmer and Townshend not to attempt it. He did not suggest an altern-ative plan ; he contented himself by saying that the proposed plan, among other faults, " would prove disastrous to the Empire."

Thus was Townshend's last chance thrown away ; and from now to the bitter end the Turks enclosed him ever tighter in their grip. Here General Sir John Nixon leaves the stage, to be succeeded by General Lake, as Army Commander in Mesopotamia.

All through the middle of January, discussions and arguments went on, and telegrams kept flying between Lake, Aylmer, and Townshend. One day Townshend would break out, if conditions were favourable : next day he couldn't possibly think of such a thing. One day the Russians were hastening to capture Baghdad ; next day they were retiring to the Caucasus.

Early in February, General Aylmer put forward the following plan : To cross to the right bank of the Tigris with the greater part of his Force, and push down against the Dujailah position (south of Kut), while his artillery hammered the Sanniyat defile, from the right bank, and pinned the Turks to their position between Sanniyat and Umm el Hannah.

It has been already mentioned that directly to the east of the Kut loop three small canals lead out of the Tigris ; the most westward being the Dujailah, just two miles from the right bank of the Tigris, opposite Kut. Aylmer's plan then was, having pushed south west along the right bank, to swing in his left between the Dujailah Canal and the Shatt el Hai, and thus get in touch with Townshend.

On receiving the report of the fight at Sheikh Saad, the Home Government took the control of the Campaign out of the hands of Indian Army Headquarters, and placed the operations in Mesopotamia under the control of the War Office. At once (Feb. 10th) Sir William Robertson sent out instructions to the effect that all efforts must be directed to the relief of Kut.

For the next week the military authorities at Home, in India, and in Mesopotamia, kept sending telegrams and cables to each other, and making wild guesses at the strength of the Turkish forces on the Tigris. Until at last, on the 19th of February, orders were definitely issued that, on the 22nd, operations were to be undertaken " with the object of causing the greatest amount of harm to the enemy " in the Hannah, or Sanniyat, defile.

Battle of Dujailah, or second Battle of Es Sinn.

The total strength of General Aylmer's force was now 18,000 infantry, 1,800 cavalry, and 66 guns. It was divided into four groups, the principal group being under the command of General Gorringe ; with a strength of 9,000 infantry, 1,300 cavalry, and 38 guns. It was to move along the right bank of the Tigris until it reached the bend of the river near Sanniyat, at a ridge, called Abu Rumman, where some Turkish trenches had been dug. Its guns were to bombard the Turkish positions on the left bank between Umm el Hannah and Sanniyat.

On the left bank were the other three groups : General Young-husband's consisting of 5,000 infantry, 250 cavalry, and 22 guns, to attack the Hannah defile ; General Norie's, on the right of this, to threaten the enemy's left flank; and General Rice, with about 1,800 infantry and two guns, to protect the camps and hold the bridges over the Tigris and Wady.

At half-past six on the morning of the 22nd, the guns of Gorringe's group began a hail of shell on the Turks in the Hannah defile. At the first shot the Turks struck their tents and rushed into the trenches at the mouth of the defile. By the afternoon General Gorringe's right had reached Abu Rumman.

About five miles to the south of this place there is a marsh, the Umm el Brahm, the terrain on each side of which was found to be suitable for the movement of all arms. On the 24th, General Gorringe's right again pushed forward about four miles, with little opposition. On the evening of the 26th, Aylmer sent a telegram to Townshend, explaining to him the plan of the forthcoming attack, so that he could act, to assist it, as he might think best.

For the next two days the rain poured, almost without intermission; and on the 1st of March it came down still worse than before.

On the 4th of March, the Army Commander, General Lake, sent a number of suggestions and comments to Aylmer, mainly to the effect that he should employ ruses similar to those of Townshend which had proved so successful at the first battle of Es Sinn. He also added that the Commander-in-Chief in India and the Chief of the Imperial General Staff were of the opinion that the attack should not be delivered until the end of March. But Aylmer's troops, who found it so difficult to march, up to their knees, in mud, by day, could not possibly carry out a night march such as a feint in front of the Turks entailed; and he considered it more advisable to attack the Turks at once than to wait until they had been strengthened by further reinforcements.

On the 3rd of March, General Aylmer issued a series of false orders, in the hope that they would be communicated to the enemy, and deceive him. They were to the effect that the force now on the right bank of the Tigris (under General Younghusband) should cross to the left bank on the night of the 5th/6th, March and attack the Hannah defile next morning. Now false orders may be sometimes successful, and lead the enemy astray; but in general they are dangerous tools that may cut the very hand which uses them; especially if they fail in gaining the object for which they were issued. A commander who gives his subordinates and troops the impression that he does not fully trust them, or that he is constantly changing his mind, cannot expect them to prepare the execution of his genuine orders with energy, resolution, or confidence.

On the 6th of March, General Aylmer issued his orders for the real attack, which was to commence on the morning of the 8th. The right flank of the Turkish position, on the right bank of the Tigris, was to be turned and rolled back to the river ; where the British troops who carried out this movement were to get in touch with Townshend, with only the river between them and Kut.

While this was being carried out, a force of 7,000 men and 24 guns, under General Younghusband, was to attack vigorously the Turkish main position in the Hannah-Sanniyat defile. This attack was to be assisted by the fire of five gunboats on the river.

General Kemball was placed in command of the force which was to operate on the right bank of the river and turn the Turkish right at the Dujailah redoubt and trenches. The strength of his force was 7,000 men and 70 guns. These he divided into two columns : " A," under General Christian, 3,000 men and six guns ; " B " under Colonel Campbell, about 4,000 men and a Field Artillery Brigade.

These columns were to be followed by the Cavalry Brigade, 1,200 sabres and four guns, under General Stephen ; while, as a sort of General Reserve, was Column " C," under General Keary, of 8,000 men and 36 guns.

About six miles south of Abu Rumman and one mile west of the Umm al Brahm marshes, there is a place which, in the orders, was called the Ruined Hut. This was to be the meeting place of Kemball's columns, which they were to reach by a march to be carried out on the night of the 7th/8th. It meant an advance for about six miles, and over open ground, of a column 160 yards wide and two miles deep.

While this movement was taking place on the right bank, the Turkish position at the Hannah defile was to be heavily bombarded by the guns of Younghusband's force.

On the night of the 7th/8th, at about 2.30 a.m., Columns "A" and " B " reached the rendezvous near the Ruined Hut. Column " C " reached the same place two hours later.

Column "A" resumed its march at half-past three in the morning ; and reached a point on the Dujailah Canal, three miles south-east from the Dujailah redoubt, shortly after five o'clock. It was followed by Column " B " at a distance of 200 yards.

The sun rose at half-past six ; when General Christian's troops could clearly see, in the north-west, the redoubt, their objective. Just then Column " C " had got into position opposite the Sinn Abtar redoubt, which was about a mile and a half to the north of the Dujailah redoubt ; and began to entrench, at a distance of about two miles from the Turkish position. Behind Column "C" came the Commander and Staff of the Tigris Corps.

At about 8 o'clock the infantry of "A" and " B " Columns advanced to the attack of the Turkish position, assisted by the fire of their guns.

Kemball ordered the 36th Brigade to swing round by the right of the Turkish trenches, and then push northwards, followed by the 28th and 9th Brigades. This movement began at about 9 o'clock, but came to a standstill shortly before 11. The Brigades entrenched themselves hastily on the ground which they had won ; while the rest of Column "A" came up in support, and Column " B " struck at the trenches south of the Dujailah Redoubt.

Thick black clouds now came up from the south-west, and heavy, rain began to fall ; during which the Turks came crowding into the trenches opposite Column "A" and west of the Dujailah Redoubt. The British Brigades could not make any headway here, notwithstanding the gallant attempts of the Devons and the Leicesters.

Severe fighting now went on until about 2 o'clock in the afternoon ; by which time the Turks had got a number of fresh guns into previously-prepared positions, with marked ranges, and devoted all their attention to the British left. "A" and " B " Columns had failed.

About half-past three, General Aylmer came up to the position of " C " Column, east of the Sinn Abtar Redoubt, and he ordered one more attempt to break the centre of the Turkish lines of defence. If now Columns "A" and " B " had been capable of giving efficient support to this attempt, it would probably have succeeded ; but they had been badly mauled, and their losses were very heavy.

Just before sunset the intensity of the Turkish rifle and gun fire increased ; and when night fell, the advanced British troops withdrew from the positions they had gained earlier in the day. They had not yet assimilated the Turkish battle tactics : allowing the enemy to come on, even into a prepared position, until he arrives exactly where he is expected and wanted ; then come down on him with full force and wipe him out.

At 7 o'clock that evening General Aylmer issued orders that a Brigade should entrench, on a frontage of about two miles, on a line about three miles east of the Dujailah lines, and that the whole force was to begin the retreat at 9 p.m. At 11 o'clock next morning what was left of the Infantry Brigades began to march back in the direction of Sheikh Saad.

The 35th Brigade, which had been ordered to entrench and place outposts, was now supported by the 7th and 8th Brigades ; the three forming a protection to the rest of the force retiring ; with another Brigade and the Cavalry Brigade as reserves.

The troops were to stand to arms at 5 a.m. on the 9th, when all transport was to be loaded and ready to move off at 7 a.m., the last of the covering troops, the 36th Brigade, moved off. The rearguard, at 6 a.m., was formed of the 9th and 28th Infantry Brigades and a Brigade (9th) of Field Artillery.

The inter-communication in the Force was very badly managed ; an important message which General Kemball should have received at 9 o'clock on the evening of the 8th did not reach him until 6.30 on the morning of the 9th.

Aylmer's casualties amounted to over 1,000 killed and 2,500 wounded ; and, with insufficient transport, he had to march fifteen miles back to the Wady, with no drinking-water on the route.

General Kemball and his troops did all that men could do, to evacuate the wounded and secure the safe retreat of the rest of the Force ; and it was not till 3 o'clock on the afternoon of the 9th that the last of them left the field of battle.

A small body of the Turks, with a few guns, followed the retreating Force for some time. A few of their shells caused a stampede among the mules of some machine-gun units, and about fifty casualties in the rearguard.

The Force reached the Tigris by midnight on the 9th. General Younghusband's Force, on the left bank, had not succeeded in expelling the Turks from the Hannah defile.

The casualties of the British in this battle were a little over 4,000 in killed, wounded, and missing ; altogether amounting to about 16 per cent. of the whole. The Turkish casualties were 3,100.

Just ten days after this, the Tigris was seized with its annual attack of bad temper—which sometimes raises it twenty feet in one night—and the melted snow from the Armenian heights began to come down in great floods, which changed the whole Tigris region into a swamp, and rendered military operations impossible.

On the 12th of March, General Gorringe succeeded Aylmer ; but the floods rose so quickly that any move against the Es Sinn position would be attended with great difficulties. Still Gorringe undertook preparations for another attack on the Hannah defile. On the 9th of April the Turks gave way before him, drawing him deeper into the defile ; then they suddenly turned on him and drove him back, with heavy loss. He then, on the 14th, sent the greater part of his force across the river, and pushed back a small body of Turks on the right bank. This seems to have encouraged him ; for he attacked the Turks again on the 23rd. They retreated : this time nearly as far back as Sanniyat ; drew him on and then turned on him, as before. He could not get near the Sanniyat trenches, in which the Turks were lying, breast to back ; nothing of them to be seen over the top of the trenches but their fingers manipulating the locks of their rifles. He was beaten ; out of his three Divisions (3rd, 7th and 13th) he had now lost nearly 5,000 men ; and he made no further attempt to get near Kut.

The futile attempts which had been made up to the present had cost the British Army not less than 25,000 men. There has never been in the whole history of the British Army any other example of such a gross violation of the principle of Economy of Force.

If, on the 8th of March, Townshend had only made a desperate dash to get across two hundred yards of water, to his brother soldiers who were within three miles of him, General Aylmer would have gained a victory at Dujailah and saved Kut. This would have been no more than the gallant Aylmer fully deserved ; for in the whole history of War no commander ever made a nobler attempt to save the troops and the reputation of a brother officer.

On the 29th of April, 1916, Kut surrendered to the Turks under Khalil Pasha, after a siege which had lasted 143 days. The British troops who surrendered numbered 2,970, and the Indian troops over 6,000.

About a week before the surrender of Kut, General Von der Goltz Pasha died at Turkish Army Headquarters. The wireless which reported this news attributed his death to what was called in the telegram *der Fleckentyphus*, spotted fever ; but the Russian wireless of a few days later stated positively that the General had been assassinated ; and that the spots on his body were caused by the bullets from the revolver of a Turkish officer whom he had degraded.

Chapter XI.

AFTER THE FALL OF KUT.

The Turkish Commanders on the Tigris were well aware that their joy over the fall of Kut was of a nature to be soon followed by weeping. They knew that they would now have to meet a hurricane from the south ; so they prepared to meet it. They began by transferring to the left bank of the Tigris nearly all the troops that had been holding the trenches opposite the Sanniyat defile, from Abu Rumman to Bait Issah. Then Gorringe sent forward a Division to take the place of these, towards the end of May.

Things remained in this state until the beginning of November, when the storm burst on them with terrific force. They had now a very strong men to deal with, General Maude. He was not going to be enticed half way into a long defile and then have his force cut up ; he was not the man to butt his head against a brick wall.

He started by clearing the Turks from the right bank of the river ; slowly, but methodically and surely. By personal reconnaissance he had carefully noted the strong points of the Sanniyat position ; and, for the present, he contented himself in bombarding it from the right bank ; keeping his eye fixed on Kut all the time, and knowing that when he got that position he would then have caught the Turks at Sanniyat like rats in a trap. He moved forward, as warily and cautiously as an elephant crossing a shaky wooden bridge ; never putting down his foremost foot until he had well tested the surface in front and knew it was strong enough to bear. His movements puzzled and mystified the enemy far more completely than the transparent tricks of Townsehnd, Aylmer, and Gorringe had done. In the words of the poet, they " never knew what he was up to next."

By the middle of December, the Turks in the Dujailah trenches were already accustomed to see, in the early morning, the bright points of the lances of a few horsemen, on the western sandhills ; and they could see that these active and quickly-moving lances were not carried by any slovenly, prowling Arabs. So they thought it better to clear out of the Dujailah position in time ; and, by the third week in January, Maude's scouts reported to him that Kut was clear of the enemy. But he was not going to take any chances. He pushed on steadily, until he was in a position to spring suddenly on Kut.

The Turks, still not appreciating the calibre of the man they had now to deal with, prepared to attack the British south of Kut, from the western side ; but Maude anticipated them ; swept them headlong out of their trenches, and chased them up the river, killing hundreds of them and taking more than 2,000 prisoners.

While he was engaged in this task, the Turks at Sanniyat began to see the trap he was about to set for them ; so they cleared out of this position on the night of the 23rd of February, and hurried back along the Baghdad road. Next day, they were joined by some fugitives from Kut and some lightly-wounded soldiers, who informed them that the new English devil, with the largest and most terrible army ever seen, had swallowed up Kut as easily as a child eats a date.

Maude kept them on the run, never for a moment letting them rest. On the 9th of March they tried to hold him up at the Diyala river ; but he brushed them aside, with heavy loss, and entered Baghdad on the 11th of March.

There is no finer or more successful piece of organisation and fighting in modern military history than this carried out by Maude. With no railway at his command, very bad roads, a tortuous river of strong currents and many shoals, and under a sweltering sun, he never stopped, day or night, until he had captured Baghdad, chased the enemy well beyond it, and filled their souls with mortal fear. He had no intention of giving time to the enemy's reinforcements north of Baghdad to get down for its defence.

Fifteen days after the fall of Kut he entered Baghdad. Even then he wasted no time. He sent out two columns ; one to the north, the other north-east. The latter, in concert with a small body of Russian troops from the Persian frontier, drove the Turks on further north.

The Turks had lost heart ; they felt themselves completely beaten ; they killed some German officers who tried to make them turn round and face the British again ; and, where they did not kill them, they cursed them loudly, from the ranks ; devoutly praying that their faces might be blackened and the graves of their fathers defiled by yellow dogs.

In the operations from April to September, 1917, Samarra, sixty-five miles north of Baghdad, was reached by Maude's columns, who, on the way, picked up 12,000 prisoners of war and 120 guns.

The most brilliant operation in Maude's Campaign was the advance from Kut to Baghdad ; a distance of 110 miles, covered in 15 days, including a whole day's fighting outside the ancient city of the Caliphs of Islam. It can be truly stated that the skilful planning and brilliant execution of this movement retrieved, in a great measure, the earlier mistakes of the Mesopotamian Campaign.

From November 1914 to November 1917, the number of men employed in the British Forces in Mesopotamia was 890,000 ; the maximum strength during this time (September 1917) was 450,000. The casualties were : killed, 35,000 ; wounded, 53,000 ; missing, 15,000 ; a total of over 100,000, which was only exceeded in France and Gallipoli.

When the news of Townshend's surrender became known in England, Uncle Pumblechook, who had foretold " a good prospect of final success for the brilliant operations," now stated, in the House of Commons, that the fall of Kut was " a matter of no military significance whatever " ; yet, to keep on the right side of public opinion, he instituted a " Commission of Inquiry," to take evidence on alleged misdemeanours.

Oh, those Commissions ! A brief acquaintance with such Commissions enables anyone, from the name and character of the individuals composing them, to anticipate their report, almost word for word ; for not only are the witnesses prejudiced who give evidence before the Commission, but these same witnesses frequently get very broad hints beforehand as to the nature of the evidence expected from them.

The Report of the Mesopotamian Commission was published on the 27th of June, 1917 ; and, on the 18th of July, the House of Commons showed their opinion, and their good sense, by deciding that they did not want to hear anything more about it.

Chapter XII.

KUT TO BAGHDAD.

When the British military authorities and politicians had first decided to carry out an operation, in the Turkish case, they proceeded like a surgeon who carefully cuts the corns on the patient's foot before amputating the leg. This was because they could not or would not see that the only effective cure was to lop off the limb. Of all those who dealt with the case, there were only two who had foresight enough to grasp this fact : Lord Crewe and Sir William Robertson. The latter showed that he was endowed with the rare gift of being a good judge of men ; and he selected the very best man to perform the operation. This man was *Maude.*

After Kut had fallen, and all through May and June, the heat went on increasing in the Tigris plain, until, by the end of July, it became so terrific that both Turk and British found it hard enough to keep alive ; when a man clapped his hand to the lock of his rifle the skin of his palm stuck to it as if he had touched red-hot iron. For the present both sides had had enough of fighting ; their losses were great ; they were exhausted ; and they tacitly agreed to an irregular, unofficial armistice.

The Secretary of State for War, Lord Kitchener, ordered General Lake to stand on the defensive for the present ; but, at the same time, to keep his force pushed forward as far as possible, consistent with safety ; for we could not afford to fall back down the Tigris.

The strength of the Tigris Corps, under General Gorringe, was now three Divisions, three Infantry Brigades, and one Cavalry Brigade ; in all, about 28,000 men and 140 guns. The force on the Euphrates at the same time was three Squadrons of Cavalry, nine Battalions of Infantry, and four Batteries of Artillery.

General Lake's first efforts, during the hot weather of 1916, were directed to bring Gorringe's force up to full strength, to supply it with sufficient transport, and to see that it did not lose touch with the enemy.

This policy and these efforts were approved by the Chief of the Imperial General Staff, who put forward the idea that a strong and agressive British Force on the Tigris would have the effect of containing in front of it a large Turkish Force, and keep this from sending reinforcements back to Baghdad, to defend this city against a Russian Force now moving westwards from the Persian frontier. But the Russian Force proved only a broken reed ; and, except for the purpose of influencing Turkish plans, the idea of practical co-operation between British and Russian was an empty and unprofitable one. On the 20th of May a handful of Russians, about 120 strong, came to Ali el Gharbi, having got over a difficult march of about 200 miles ; and they were received in the British Camp with an enthusiasm and joy almost as great as if they had been the advanced guard of a victorious Allied Army. For all the practical good they effected they might have stayed with their own force, which, a week afterwards, was soundly beaten by the Baghdad Turkish Force, and hunted back all the way to Hamadan.

The Turks in front of Gorringe were strongly entrenched at Sanniyat and Bait Issah (two miles south-west of Sanniyat, on the right bank of the Tigris). Their strength here was about 20,000 men and 60 guns ; between Kut and Baghdad, about 6,000. All the Turkish Forces in Mesopotamia were now under the command of General Halil Pasha, who had succeeded General Von der Goltz.

About the middle of May a new Division was formed, under General Egerton, at the advanced base, Shaikh Saad, and a strong boat bridge was laid across the river here. We had now one division on the left bank, and five brigades on the right bank. The aeroplanes with the Force were inferior to those used by the Turks.

The Force on the right bank kept pushing forward steadily ; moving at a distance of about five miles south of the river ; brushing aside all opposition, and giving a very short shrift to treacherous, prowling Arabs ; until, by the end of the first week in June, they mastered and occupied the mounds and trenches between the once formidable Dujailah Redoubt and Imam al Mansur, five miles south-east of Kut.

Behind, following the track of this Force, came the light railway ; protected by barbed wire and detached posts, 17 miles long, from the Shaikh Saad bridge to what was the right flank of the old Es Sinn position, four miles south of the river and seven miles east of the Kut loop. This light railway was completed by September, 1916 ; and in the meantime another light railway had been laid from Basra to Nasiriyeh, up the Euphrates.

Notwithstanding these efforts, carried out under great climatic disadvantages, General Gorringe reported to General Lake, in the middle of June, that the Tigris Corps was absolutely incapable of assuming the offensive, owing to sickness, especially cholera, which was ravaging in his camp. He had not less than 22,000 casualties during April and May.*

Still fresh British troops kept coming up to the front, until, by the middle of July, the strength of the Tigris Corps was 100,000, of whom 40,000 were British. Earlier in the month General Gorringe's health completely gave way ; and, on the 11th the Tigris Corps came under the command of General Maude.

In the beginning of August, General Lake felt that he could no longer support the great difficulties and anxieties of the Campaign; so General Maude was appointed to fill his place, while the command of the Tigris Corps was committed to General Cobbe. From the 28th of August, Maude was Commander-in-Chief in Mesopotamia.

On the 22nd of August, General Robertson, in giving a short review of the situation, stated that by the end of October we should have in Mesopotamia a total force of 52,000 infantry, 5,000 cavalry, and 228 guns. The Commander-in-Chief, in India, wished to commence operations with this force at once ; but the cautious and experienced old soldier, Robertson, put the brake on, and would hear nothing of the offensive till everything was ready for the tiger's spring.

On the 12th September, in a telegram to the Commander-in-Chief in India, and to General Maude, he said : " I am considering withdrawal to Amarah, with increase of force at Ahwaz, and a strong central reserve in the Basra-Ahwaz area, ready to act, either north, west, or east. This plan would safeguard oilfields, and command both rivers." This is very like the plan suggested by Townshend, which was at once rejected by Nixon.

But Maude would not hear of falling back from his present front ; and Maude was right. He seems to have been, at this time, the only man east of Suez who could see farther than his own nose. Here, the official account of the War,† as far as Mesopotamia was concerned, reads like the description of a game of " forfeits," or " consequences," played by a week-end party of revellers in a country mansion.

" On the 19th September the Chief of the Imperial General Staff informed Sir Beauchamp Duff and General Maude that until General Monro had discussed the question with Generals Skeen

---

*In June the casualties amounted to 11,000, in July, 12,000, and in August, 11,000 men.

†*History of the War*, vol. iii, p. 46.

and Richardson, and then with General Kirkpatrick, no definite instructions could be issued."

Can anybody imagine a Napoleon, a Wellington, a Marlborough, a Moltke, or a Foche, having anything to do with this silly " House that Jack built " game ? Surely it was nothing short of a miracle which prevented the broth from being not only spoiled but poisonous, with all these cooks !

In the end, however, Maude had his way. On the last day of September, Sir William Robertson wired to him* : " I wish you to understand that so far as I personally am concerned, I leave it entirely to your judgment." General Monro, the new Commander-in-Chief in India, also gave Maude his benediction in nearly the same form. He came to Basra about the middle of October ; and, after having discussed various plans, "summed up " by stating that the existing position was "the one best calculated to carry out the instructions of H.M. Government and to uphold our prestige."

Maude's strategy in the meantime was to secure command of the right bank of the Tigris ; first, from Shaikh Saad to the Shatt al Hai ; secure the Hai River ; dart from here on to the Shumran loop (five miles west of Kut) ; and, crossing to the left bank higher up the river, to cut the communications of the Turkish Forces, which still held on between Kut and Sanniyat. All through November he was making preparations to carry this plan into effect.

By the 11th of December he had completed his concentration on the Tigris front. His Air Force was greatly improved ; he had nothing to fear from the Euphrates direction on the west, because General Brooking had given a sound thrashing to the Muntafik Arabs at Nasiriyeh in the second week in September. Above all else he took the greatest care to secure sufficient transport for his force ; so that he should be no longer tied down to the river, but could move with plenty of supplies at a considerable distance away from it.

On the left bank of the Tigris, between Kut and Sanniyat, the Turks had 20,000 men and 70 guns ; on the right bank, just south of the Kut (or Khudaira) bend, they had 3,000 men and 15 guns, holding the northern reach of the Hai. There was only a distance of about two miles here between them and the advanced British Force.

---

*History of the War, vol. iii, p. 48.

Maude's strength was 45,000 infantry, 3,500 cavalry and 174 guns. He took care that the light railway kept close to his heels, and it reached the Hai, at Atab, by the end of January, 1917.

The forward movement began in the night of the 13th/14th December, carried out by the 1st and 3rd Army Corps. The 1st Corps consisted of the 3rd and 7th Divisions; they were partly on the left bank, facing the Sanniyat position, and stretching on their left nearly to the Dujailah Canal. The 3rd Corps, consisting of the 13th and 14th Divisions, was extended south-west of the 1st Corps, with its outposts on the Hai, eight miles south of the Kut loop.

Early in the morning of the 14th, the cavalry and three infantry brigades of the 3rd Corps crossed the Hai, near Atab, with very little opposition. The cavalry pushed out towards the Shumran bend, and found it strongly held. The 1st Corps bombarded the Sanniyat position during the whole day (14th) and made as if they were about to force a passage to the left bank, between Sanniyat and Kut.

On the 15th the 3rd Corps gained ground towards the Kut bend, and some brigades on the left of the 1st Corps came on behind them.

On the 17th and 18th they pushed slowly westwards; Maude's intentions being to pin the Turks to their ground between Kut and Sanniyat; then to cross to the left bank and cut their communications.

About six miles west of the Shumran bend is the Husaini bend, which was reached by our Cavalry Brigade on the 20th.

Bombardments and slow movements along the right bank continued up to the 24th; by which time the line of the Hai was entirely in Maude's hands. From this date until the end of the first week in January, the British Force kept creeping nearer to Kut and securing their gains.

The attack on Kut itself took place on the 9th of January, and continued for two days. It was not quite successful; the fierce and stubborn fighting of the Turks came as an unpleasant surprise to some of our commanders.

The next week was occupied in consolidating the ground gained, and on the 21st of January another attack took place. The rains came down and made movement slow and difficult. Sluggish operations marked the first weeks of February; till, at length, on the 24th of this month, Kut surrendered to General Maude. On the evening of this day he wrote: " As a result of our operations we have now the whole of the enemy's positions from

Sanniyat to Kut ; and Kut itself, to which no interest but a senti-mental one attaches, passes automatically into our hands, though we have not yet actually occupied it. We have also secured navi-gation of the river up to Shamran."

The first difficulty after this was the clearing of the Shumran bend, on the west of Kut, a task which was carried out by the 1st Corps. The attack was led by the 38th Brigade (all British) ; but, owing to the very heavy fire from the well-sited Turkish trenches, especially on the right bank, by the old Massag Canal, the assailants were completely held up on the afternoon of the 25th, until the 39th Brigade dashed up to support them, and the Turks gave way. As the Turks retired they naturally became stronger and stronger ; for the retreating soldiers packed those trenches which had been only lightly held before ; and the tasks of the British soldiers became more and more difficult. A strange stroke of ill-luck here befel the gallant North Staffordshires, of the 39th Brigade. They had captured a number of prisoners just when the other Turks from the trenches dashed out in a counter-attack ; then the captured men, taking advantage of the confusion, and being lightly guarded, picked up rifles and cartridges, and attacked the Staffordshires in rear. This was more than the Stafford-shires could stand ; so they were compelled to fall back from the position they had so gallantly carried only a few hours before. Then the Gloucesters came up on their right ; they all advanced again ; kept up the fight till 2 o'clock next morning, when they at length got into the position, where they found only dead and dying Turks. The 38th and 39th Brigades of the 13th Division had lost 600 men.

To the west of the Husaini bend are Iman Mahdi and Shaikh Jaad, on the left bank, and Bughaila on the right, further on. At Imam Mahdi the Turks tried to make another stand ; but General Crocker and his cavalry were down on them like a flash before they had time to make themselves at home in their new position ; and he swept them before him, keeping them on the run for about twelve miles, until they reached a roughly-prepared position at the Nahr al Kalek bend. This cavalry operation was supported by the 3rd Corps ; while the 1st Corps, in rear, chastised the maraud-ing Arabs, who flocked like carrion crows on the left of our advance.

On the 26th, the flotilla on the Tigris played a most important part in the pursuit. At Nahar al Kalek, Captain Nunn, in com-mand, was able to see which was the main body of the retreating Turks, and which their rearguard. Nunn showered shells on the rear of the main body, so that they ran like hares before him ; he then turned his attention to the rearguard, many of whom were seen to throw down their rifles and headgear, and raise their arms, begging to be saved from the Arabs who had now come in among them and were cutting their throats like sheep in the shambles.

This, the 26th, is an important date ; because, shortly after nightfall, the Turkish Commander-in-Chief, Halil Pasha, hastened back to Baghdad, and sent begging telegrams to all his brother commanders, to tell them that if they did not come quickly to help him he would not attempt to defend Baghdad. His supply system had broken down, which he attributed to the laziness and cowardice of his German personnel.

On the evening of the 27th, the advanced cavalry had got within a few miles of Aziziyeh, and the 3rd Corps was about Sharqui, three miles north-east of the Nahr al Kalek bend. On the advice of General MacMunn, I.G. Communications, General Maude decided to make a halt, to give time for sufficient supplies to come up. The 1st Corps stood at Shaikh Jaad, twelve miles south-east of the 3rd Corps. The Force remained in these positions until the 4th of March. Then the Cavalry Division and 3rd Corps concentrated at Aziziyah, where Maude also established his headquarters. With fourteen aeroplanes the R.A.F. maintained touch with the enemy.

From here, on the 2nd of March, Maude sent a telegram to the Chief of the Imperial General Staff, in which he stated his intention to enter Baghdad with a cavalry division and four infantry divisions. He added that his occupation of Baghdad would have the following advantages : (1) enable us to organise local sources of supply on the Tigris and Euphrates ;* (2) gain control of the Euphrates below Baghdad ; (3) by a firm attitude, preserve order all along our communications.

He started out from Aziziyeh on the 5th of March, in the following order : Naval Flotilla and Cavalry Division, objective Lajj ; 3rd Corps to Zeur ; leading Division of 1st Corps to Aziziyeh. He did not expect to meet any serious resistance before reaching the Diyala river ; but about midday (on the 5th) his cavalry had a smart skirmish with a Turkish rearguard force at Zeur, where the 13th Hussars added fresh glory to their battle honors. Next day the cavalry pushed on to Bawi, six miles south of the junction of the Diyala and Tigris ; and now Maude decided to push on the 3rd Corps close up behind the cavalry, to secure a crossing over the Diyala.

---

*The Euphrates, near Falluja, is within 25 miles of Baghdad.

On the afternoon of the 7th, General Marshall, with the leading division of the 3rd Corps, having arrived within two miles of the Diyala near its junction with the Tigris, decided to cross it during the night, and reported his intention to Maude; upon which Maude now pushed up the I. Corps to Bawi, and sent a small force across to the right bank, with orders to push up to the Shaikh Aswad bend, and attract the attention of the Turks from the crossing of the Diyala.

First of all, an attempt was made to lay a pontoon bridge across the Diyala, here about 120 yards wide; but this proved a failure; because the Turkish sharpshooters on the other side, aided by the bright moonlight, picked off the men who were carrying the pontoons every time they approached the riverside.

All through this night they heard loud explosions in the direction of Baghdad, and saw reflected in the sky the sheen of the burning buildings in the city. This induced Maude to believe that the Turks would make no serious attempt to defend Baghdad. He sent his Cavalry Division across the Bawi bridge to the right bank. This was to be followed by the leading division of the 1st Corps, and push on to Baghdad.

An attempt to cross the Diyala, on the night of the 8th/9th, was again a failure, though a small party of the North Lancashires, about 100 strong, had effected a lodging on the right bank, where they dug themselves in.

On the right bank of the Tigris, and about a mile south-west from Baghdad, is the Railway Station; and nearly two miles south of this is the western hairpin bend of Karada, and Karada Island. Stretching north-west of this for nearly five miles, are the Umm al Tubul sandhills, which reach the shallow lake Aquarquf, from the south-western corner of which the Mahsudiya Canal runs to the Tigris, joining it opposite Karada Island. A narrow gauge railway ran from near the Railway Station to the south-west, crossing this canal by the "Iron Bridge," and cutting through the Umm al Tubul sandhills. The main line ran from the station to the north-west, roughly parallel to the course of the Tigris; and, five miles north-west of Baghdad is the first important station on it, Kadhimain. The Tigris and Diyala form a large salient with the vertex pointing south, terminating at the village of Diyala. Five miles north-west of this we come to the village of Quarara, on the direct road from the south to Baghdad; and two miles north-east of Quarara there are the sandy mounds, called Tel Mohammed. From these mounds a road, four miles long, ran north-west, crossing the Nazim Pasha Embankment, and entering Baghdad from the south-east. There is an old em-

bankment running almost south from the point where the narrow
gauge railway above-mentioned cuts the Umm al Tubul sandhills; it is called Tel Aswad, "the black heap." Opposite the
middle of this heap, and three miles east of it is Shawa Khan,
through which a rough road ran, from the south, up to the Iron
Bridge.

About 9 o'clock on the morning of the 9th, General Davies,
commanding the 28th Infantry Brigade of the 7th Division, sent
forward the Leicesters against the Black Heap. They encountered
a heavy fire from the mounds, and dug themselves in. Then
the Sikhs came up, on the west of Shawa Khan, to assist in the
Leicester attack; but they were held up too. Then General Fane,
commanding the 7th Division, came up with all his guns; and this
move caused the Turkish Commander to believe that the main
attack on Baghdad was to come from the right bank of the Tigris.
So, as quickly as possible, he began to move men and guns from
the Diyala salient to the right bank; which was the very worst
thing he could have done; because the troops on the move to
assist him did not get to him in time to be of any use, and the
salient was stripped of its defenders. He played exactly the game
which suited his opponent, Maude; and Maude was the very
last man with whom he should have attempted to play such a
game.

Fane made no progress during the afternoon and night of the
9th; and he was justified in complaining that he had got but very
little assistance from the Cavalry Division. On the next morning
General Maude took the cavalry, acting independently, under
his own direct orders. On the night of the 9th/10th, the 13th Division
succeeded in crossing the Diyala, by pontoons, in two columns;
and, on the afternoon of the 10th, when they reached the Quarara-
Tel Mohammed line of trenches, they could see to the north the
clouds of dust which marked the Turkish columns hastening back
to Baghdad.

Early on the morning of the 10th, Fane pushed forward his
troops. The elements proved in favour of the old Chinese cam-
paigner in this, his last great fight; for a regular hurricane burst
from the south-west, in the backs of his men, but driving thick
black dust and light gravel into the eyes of the unfortunate Turks
at Umm al Tubul. By 2 o'clock in the afternoon he had completely
swept the Turks out of their position and clean across the Mahsudiya
Canal. He entered Baghdad from the west, next morning.

All through the night of the 10th/11th, the Turkish columns
retreated out of Baghdad along the roads and tracks leading

northwards ; and Maude, on the left bank of the river, met with no opposition in his entry to the Ancient City of the Caliphs, on the morning of the 11th. The Turkish Force defending it had a strength of 15,000 men and 50 guns ; Maude's Force was about 50,000 strong with 180 guns.

A Turkish military historian* writes in most complimentary terms of the good discipline, the excellent conduct, and the humanity of the British troops on the occasion of the fall of Baghdad.

But this is nothing new to those who know the honorable and glorious history of the British Army. Just a century ago, Marshal St. Cyr, wrote :—†

"From time to time, in war and in peace, the nations of Europe have acted against us treacherously, meanly (*vilement*), sometimes barbarously, often most dishonorably ; Prussians, Spaniards, Saxons, Austrians, Italians and Russians ; all Europeans, all of them, with one remarkable exception—the British. From the English only, as soldiers, in war, we have always experienced hard blows, but fair dealing and honorable treatment : I feel it my duty to place this on record."

MAY SUCH BE ALWAYS THE VERDICT OF OUR ALLIES, OF OUR ENEMIES, AND OF HISTORY !

---

*Mohammed Amin.
†*Memoirs*, vol. iii, p. 186.

BAGHDAD
Diala
Sulman Pak
(CTESIPHON
RUINS)
Azizie
Hamidie
R. TIGRIS
BABIL-
BABYLON
Hilla
Baghela
KUT AL AMARA
Shadie
Samaika
Marsh
Wadi
Umm-el-Hannah
Shaikh
Saad
Ali-el-
Gharbi
Kut el Hai
Tisien
Shatt el Hai
Abu Sidre
AMARAH
Iman Hamza
Kala
Rumetha
ElMatuna
Samawa
HUNTAFIK ARABS
Ezra's Tomb
NASIRIYEH
L.Hokeike
Azzam
KURNA
R. EUPHRATES
Hadi
R. EUPHRATES
Riyan
BASRA
Zobeir
Sheiba
Barjisiyah
Shamie
Shuster
Kala-i-Raga
Abi-i-Diz
Disful
AHWAZ
R. KARUN
Hawaizeh
Mezera
Mohammerah
Abadan
Fao
Budmen Id.
BENI LAM ARABS
MOHAMMED ARABS
KAB ARABS
P E R S I A
MESOPOTAMIA.

N

Scale of Miles.
MILES 50   25   0   25

PERSIAN
GULF

INDEX.

A.

www.ingramcontent.com/pod-product-compliance
Lightning Source LLC
LaVergne TN
LVHW051748080426
835511LV00018B/3270